PASSION

ANDY MURRAY

INTRODUCTION

ANDY MURRAY WAS MAKING HEADLINES

It's a question that a lot of us have thought about. Would we immediately recognize the brilliance of undeveloped, youthful talent if we came across it in person? and completely comprehend the significance of what we had seen?

8-year-old Andy Murray

If a young Chris Hoy had been racing down the track at Meadowbank Velodrome, would we have halted in our tracks? Or perhaps a young Kenny Dalglish, age 10, twirling and whirling on the salmon-pink shale pitches of Glasgow's East End?

I went to the Waverley Tennis Club in Edinburgh's south side on a gloomy day in April 1994 to cover the Waverley Junior Open, a Scottish ranking competition.

I was looking for players from Edinburgh and the Lothians who were making their mark as the Evening News tennis correspondent. But I still had 200 words to file and all the local players had been defeated or weren't set to play.

Big win for Andrew, 6

by Gordon Scott

TENNIS REPORTER

SIX-YEAR-OLD Andrew Murray became the youngest player to win a match in a Scottish ranking tournament yesterday when he reached the second round of the 12-and-under singles at the Waverley Junior Open.

The Dunblane ace, whose mother, then Judith Erskine, was Scottish Champion in 1981, displayed remarkable tactical awareness to oust Cults' Ryan Openshaw (11) 6-1, 6-4. He now plays the eighth seed, Andrew Hawke (Thistle).

The youngest player left in the girls' event, Perth's Elena Baltacha, the ten-year-old daughter of Inverness Caley manager Sergei

This was the epitome of a terrible day for news.

Then, on a backcourt during the 12-and-under boys' singles match, I spotted Andrew Murray. He was hardly taller than his racquet, and the tennis ball was practically bouncing off the smooth astroturf court above his head.

Even at that young age, Andy was full of anxiety and self-doubt.

He was upset with himself for making errors or failing to live up to his own absurdly high standards, and he occasionally received taunts from bystanders for his unreasonable competitiveness.

Murray chased down every ball and refused to give up.

What he lacked in height and power, he made up for by returning every ball and positioning it just where his opponent didn't want it to be. This is why I said that he had "displayed extraordinary tactical understanding."

Sounds recognizable?

The same tenacity and tactical understanding come to mind whenever I watch Andy play, including last week at the O2 against Kei Nishikori and Milos Raonic.

Judy Murray tweeted Andy Murray's first-ever newspaper article from the Edinburgh Evening News.

The outcome? a 6-1, 6-4 victory that Ryan Openshaw, who lost, afterward referred to as "embarrassing," but has since been able to put in perspective!

It was just a terrific story, pure and simple: the six-year-old son of a former Scottish women's champion defeating a much older child. I shouldn't have concentrated on Andy at all, but I did.

I believe that part of me also wanted to save the headline as a piece for my scrapbook, just in case.

I recognized Judy since she had previously won a championship, and we both sat on the club's balcony together.

She was happy with the outcome but forbade me from speaking with the winner. Even yet, he was just six.

Judy "outed" me on social media this week as the writer who handed her younger son his first newspaper headline 22 years ago.

It made me wonder: Did I know at the time that I was seeing the development of real greatness?

Not. Even Judy admitted (at least in public) that it was impossible to foresee what lay ahead. Andrew Hawke of Edinburgh defeated the young Andrew in the following round of the Open, but a year later, when he was seven years old, Andrew won the under-14s competition.

It would be oversimplified to claim that he never looked back.

Jamie was seen as the superior potential at the time.

I agreed and convinced him to play with me in a handicap doubles match in North Berwick while Andy paired up with his father Willie. He was nine years old at the time.

But looking back, what I saw in Andy that day at Waverley 22 years ago was a dedicated and single-minded young lad who wasn't going to give up without a fight, even if he didn't go on to become the finest tennis player on the globe

Andy Murray Inspired By Memories Of Ending Grand-Slam Jinx 10 Years On

Andy Murray has expressed his joy at finally breaking his grand-slam curse, which he says has plagued him for the past ten years since the ferocious late-night match that changed his image.

Even though Murray is now best remembered for his two Wimbledon victories, his most significant moment came in the 2012 US Open final, where he battled Novak Djokovic for over five hours before finally winning in five unpredictable sets.

There was a magnificent night in New York, one that kept Flushing Meadows attendees seated far into one in the morning. Murray also experienced a coming-of-age moment as he broke a run of four losses in major finals.

His long-awaited promotion to "grand-slam champion" status allowed him to put years of public scrutiny and personal uncertainty on hold.

This past weekend, Murray told reporters while seated in a café area outside Arthur Ashe Stadium, "That was a significant moment for me. "There was a lot of expectation on me to try and win that [first grand-slam championship]. Because of the inquiries I had been receiving about winning slams, most of what I had accomplished in my career up to that point seemed, at least to me, to be rather unimportant.

"Am I up to par? Am I in shape? Is my mental capacity sufficient? Like, a lot of inquiries spread out over time. And yes, it was wonderful to finally be able to move on from that since it's not useful. In addition, the guys I was up against may have all been excellent players at the time, but it may not be how people currently perceive them.

At least on the men's side, they are regarded as the top three tennis players of all time. I was aware that winning slams during this period wasn't simple. I understood that. I doubt that everyone else was, though.

Pictures from September 10, 2012, depict a bouffant-haired, wide-eyed Murray struggling against the most obstinate of opponents and a windy wind. What then does the man himself recall about that crazy night?

"I know how I felt before the match," he responded.I can still clearly recall being alone myself in the locker room, feeling anxious, lonely, and under a lot of pressure. I recall returning to the court after the contest before leaving the location and just kind of being out there once again. I don't recall if my wife left the court quickly after the game or not. But after doing a few press-related tasks here and there, I believe I walked back outside. Yes, I simply wanted to be outside by myself. I was proud of myself at the time, and I also felt very at ease. I wasn't in the mood to party wildly. I was not feeling like

After Wimbledon in 2013, I felt rather worn out and flat. From what I recall, I didn't feel that way. It was simply such a huge relief to cross that line, and I felt fairly at ease.

"These days, I hardly ever give it any thought in my regular life. I occasionally recall when someone asked me about it, but I don't give it much thought daily. Yes, it does seem like a long time ago. Since then, a lot has transpired in my life, including undoubtedly far more significant events.

The presence of Ivan Lendl, who was still in his first season as Murray's coach, was a key element in that US Open victory. Despite having previously told reporters, "I don't use any technique - I suck at it," Murray has always felt more assured thanks to Lendl's mere presence. Consequently, it is encouraging to announce that Old Stoneface will be back in New York this week, prepared to look down from the stands in his trademark ominous manner.

Before playing Argentina's Francisco Cerundulo, the 24th seed, in Monday's opening match at Louis Armstrong Stadium, Murray must solve a mystery.

All four of the competitions he competed in this summer in the US were marred by crippling cramping. To determine whether a physical imbalance is the cause of these enigmatic symptoms, he underwent sweat testing last week. But the outcomes revealed he was in excellent health.

Blood and sweat tests both came up positive, according to Murray. "No ailments. I believe that if you were lacking in one item, that would be good. Then perhaps you might argue that is the reason behind it. But at least I now know that it is more likely tied to either conditioning, hydration, or diet. I have some degree of influence over it as well. But the fact that I feel in quite a good shape makes it worrying. I'm not entirely sure why that took place. Recently, I have felt a little better during practice. I'm hoping I'll be fine on Monday.."

DON'T BE SAD FOR ME! I HAVE PASSION IN DOING THIS – NO ONE'S FORCING ME TO PLAY'

Is he there or not? In a flash, one of the best active sportsmen from Britain, Andy Murray, tells me he'll be back at Wimbledon this month, competing well in the competition that helped him become famous. Then, the following time, he sounds less confident. During a break in training, he remarks, "The test is being on the court with the top players, and it's something that, right now, is tough to provide a firm response to."

The unpredictable nature of sport is what makes it fun, but Murray isn't bringing it up. He cannot rely on his body since it has undergone such extreme stress and strain throughout his career, but especially in the last few years. He honestly has no idea what it is capable of.

Still, he has hope. He exclaims, "Yes, I feel terrific!" and has a great appearance—bright eyes, clean skin, and a composed demeanor. His shirt is dark blue Scottish. "I hope to be in good shape and able to play, and I believe I will. My team, the physiotherapists, and the physicians believe that I will. I'm eager to compete at Wimbledon once more in front of spectators. I've been missing it.

Even so... "Over the last few years, whenever someone has asked me how I feel, I have always said, "Yes, I feel fantastic! After then, something occurs.

Something indeed happens.

If you were to review Murray's recent history, you may conclude that someone (perhaps Novak Djokovic) has an Andy Murray doll and has been poking holes in it. This is especially true of his right hip, which has been the source of his problems. . At the Australian Open two years ago, his suffering was so severe that he appeared to be finished. He sobbed when asked, "How have you been feeling?" at a pre-tournament press conference. Not fantastic, he said, running out of things to say. He was in tears and had to leave the room.

When he came back, he expressed his desire to play until Wimbledon and then quit, adding, "But also, I'm not sure I'm able to accomplish that." He then became angry once more, fumbling with the rim of his cap to control his feelings. It was heartbreaking to witness. He was sad to be forced to terminate his spectacular career in the sport he had loved his entire life at the age of 31.

Then a miracle happened! He underwent extensive hip resurfacing surgery less than three weeks later and decided to keep playing and battle his way back. It hasn't been simple. He has both won and lost games. He has now contracted Covid, sustained further wounds, and watched his position in the global rankings fall from fourth to 120th. All this after having accomplished so much previously. His accomplishments are forever documented. You can't help but wonder why you would even attempt to attend Wimbledon. Why would he subject his wounded body to such pressure?

Some individuals, Murray is aware, believe he should continue to be retired. He frequently receives inquiries about it from both the press and regular customers. Even though he has stopped using social media, he is aware. He continues, his words flowing out quickly, "There are a lot of people asking me to stop playing tennis, that it's sad, and they don't want to see me playing like this, and he can't keep fit, and he can't do this, why is he still doing this?" And I tell them, "Don't be sorry for me! Nobody is pressuring me. Sport is a peculiar thing. People appear to be clamoring for you to quit doing what you love and retire."

At Queen's in 2011.

Murray, he's a lovely guy to chat to. He is straightforward and careful because he dislikes being misunderstood, but he's also willing to laugh, talk about his parenting philosophy, and crack deadpan jokes about line calls and VAR. Years ago,

18

he refused to interact with the media; instead, he simply offered one-liners and oozed anger. Who, though, hasn't evolved since their adolescent years? He looks optimistic despite all of his physical issues. When I offer the inevitable "How do you feel?" Melino's wool-made new Castore outfit he developed is being teased, but he's at ease enough to handle it: "I worked out in it, and it was incredibly wonderful and comfy. It functions. mellow enough to discuss the prospect of skipping Wimbledon: Naturally, I'd be devastated. My goal is to compete in these major competitions, which is why I practice so diligently.

On paper, Murray's chances of winning Wimbledon again are quite slim. We are aware of this, but when he plays, we also know that his supporters will secretly wish for him to win. Isn't that what sports are all about? fighting against insurmountable odds. He might, too, doesn't he? He will never truly know how talented he is unless he participates in a prestigious tournament while healthy. "It's pretty tough to assess whether I'm playing with someone who is, let's say, rated 300th in the world," he explains.

2013 Wimbledon champion. He must take on the top seeds. You can't just call them up to throw a couple of balls around, regrettably. Before the Italian Open in May, Murray did take on Djokovic in a warm-up match in Rome. "I played well; I was pleased with how I performed. It was really useful since you get more knowledge about your game. I found it enjoyable. He ponders for a while. "I don't recall the last time I engaged in a competitive match with Djokovic. It happened in Doha, I believe, around the beginning of 2017.

Although it has been a while, he still sees himself in the mix. He claims that when he practices with the best players, his standards for himself are still as high as they were when he was 20. "Even if I think back, it seems like, 'OK, you haven't played many games recently, you've been injured...' Even while I know I should have somewhat lower expectations coming into those practice matches, once I start playing, I still become impatient. For me, it has always been the situation. If you want to succeed or compete at the greatest level, I believe it is crucial to be in a rush. You must adopt that attitude to succeed in sports.

Ah, the attitude. It is crucial in elite sports. Due to their obsession with minute aspects that the average person can't get excited about, it may make champions a little boring. They have an odd, distant, and logical attitude about their bodies. Andy's body isn't his own, as Murray's wife Kim has acknowledged. It's a business, and other people have been involved: his sponsors, physiotherapists, and fans.

His colleagues raised him after the 2015 Davis Cup victory.

Murray has a history of treating his body like a tool. He distinguishes between pain and fitness, for example. He claims that all current and December physical testing demonstrates that his physical condition is the best it has ever been. But discomfort or injury limits your capacity to compete. I put in a lot of effort and maintain a healthy lifestyle so that after I overcome the worst of these issues, I can still compete at the greatest level. He exercises constantly so that he may resume training at the top as soon as the discomfort subsides.

But now, it seems like there are constant challenges, even away from his hip. He had done his finest training in the previous two years and was prepared for the Australian Open this year. He afterward revealed a positive Covid-19 test result. He felt terrible.

Playing In 2001 At The Age Of 13

He says, "I couldn't believe it. "Because I'd followed the appropriate procedures. I was scheduled to compete in a competition in Florida, but I opted not to go because it would have required travel and there were many instances nearby. I was therefore only present at my home and the National Tennis Center. Since I drive an electric vehicle, I wasn't buying gas and interacting with others in that way. I thought I had handled things perfectly. It also went badly. He cited the NTC's Covid precautions as the cause ("There were a lot of people in the gym") and expressed his anger at having not only missed the competition but also infected Kim, who was at the time pregnant, and their three children. "I was pissed off," he stated. I give that a lot of thought.

He withdrew from a competition in Dubai since they had a daughter as their fourth child at the beginning of March. Later that month, he was forced to withdraw from the Miami Open after injuring his groin while turning over in bed. Because nobody could identify the issue, that was also challenging. "I'm a person who appreciates clarity. I prefer to be able to pose a question and receive a clear-cut response. How do you solve an issue if you don't know what it is?

The French Open is set to start as we speak. He's not there either; this time, it's a strategic choice that will help him get ready for Wimbledon. Although he may not have played as many games as the other players, he will have more time on the turf.

Because of the epidemic, "to my knowledge, none of the players played on grass last year," he claims. I withdrew from the French Open to have more time to train on grass the year I won Wimbledon.

He halts. I'm not claiming that the result will be the same.!"

Andy Murray's stadium and stronghold are Wimbledon; it is where the British audience first met him and eventually came to adore him. He was first called a brat for being overly loud and energetic on the court. But the crowd warmed up to him as he grieved after losing to Federer in a four-set final in 2012.

Naturally, he ended up winning a year later, and after that, he started to push himself even more.

In 2016, he won nine championships, making history by being the first male player to win a grand slam (his second Wimbledon title), three Masters 1000 events, the ATP finals, and Olympic gold all in the same year. In 2015, he guided Great Britain to its first Davis Cup victory in 79 years. He received a knighthood, was named the world's best male singles player, and was awarded Sports Personality of the Year.

And he accomplished all of this despite a chronic hip ache that developed after a taxing match against Sam Querrey at Wimbledon in 2017. He gave it a rest, but it had no effect. He was unable to walk, let alone play tennis. He was the best in the world, yet he struggled to put his socks on. He underwent surgery on his hip at the beginning of January 2018 to remove a ligament, fix damaged cartilage, and scrape out some inflammation. With his little crew, he began months of lonesome rehabilitation (two physios, one coach). It didn't, though. By August 2018, he was sobbing uncontrollably on the court. While in misery, he had recently defeated Marius Copil in Washington. He cried while sitting in his chair with a towel over his face. He added, "I feel like this is the end." It was during the press conference in Australia a few months later.

He now admits, "I was done with tennis." "I wasn't enjoying it at all," she said. His mother wasn't so convinced he'd be content living at home with his children as his father was. Soon after, he began learning more about retired player Bob Bryan's hip resurfacing procedure. Maybe he could follow in his footsteps? Murray did just that a short while later, towards the end of January 2019. It was amazing how well he recovered—not only could he walk, but he could also play tennis. The agonizing anguish has subsided.

It's not ideal, but it does the job. Your body has been accustomed to moving in a specific manner for a very long period, he explains. Therefore, changing it by inserting a little piece of metal will alter your mobility and place tension and pressure on other areas of your body. I thus anticipated difficulty. The biomechanics are a little out of whack. But it did feel nice. He started playing again in the spring of 2019. He and Feliciano Lopez won the doubles match at Queen's. He played mixed doubles with Serena Williams at Wimbledon, where he was planning to retire, and advanced to the third round. He returned.

With him on this excruciating ride were his admirers.

He doesn't make it appear simple, which is arguably one of the reasons we should adore him. He has never been one of those athletes who easily overcome challenges. Murray, who was a little boy when the Dunblane school shooting occurred in 1996, strives for everything, dives deep, and never gives up. His legendary mother, Judy, claims that criticism motivates him. This is demonstrated in Olivia Cappuccini's insightful 2019 documentary Resurfacing on his hip injury years. There is no laxity; he complies with all physiotherapy demands. He considers the benefits and drawbacks of each situation as well as how it will affect others. He is serious about everything.

He performs a lot of his rehabilitation exercises at his and Kim's lovely home in southwest London, which features large glass doors leading to the garden and an open-concept kitchen. He also has a gym and an indoor pool there, and he marches up and down in the water to build strength in his legs.

He is seen pounding up and down on gym equipment at ungodly hours of the morning.

He appears to be at his most at ease while taunting his physios or playing with his kids in his little moments of free time. The oldest child, a male, and three girls are just five years old. I enquire about his parenting advice. Get your children into a sleep regimen as soon as you can, he advises, since if you don't, you'll be exhausted and everything will fall apart. He also advises that you attempt to see things from their perspective. Kim is reportedly excellent at doing this.

Adults frequently view things from their perspective, he claims. "For example, when their toy gets wet, we don't think it's a huge concern; you just take it home and wash it. For them, it is currently the most crucial thing in the world. Therefore, instead of dismissing their emotions when they are disturbed or sad, attempt to understand them. They seem to settle down more quickly, in my opinion.

Though we're not having any more! He loves having kids. Four is adequate. Yes, they can play doubles," he beams. When their younger brother Teddy and the infant are taking naps, he frequently watches TV with Sophia and Olivia in the middle of the day. He does it out of participation, but also because Olivia, who is three years old, can become angry about something that her bigger sister isn't disturbed by (this happened recently with Beauty And The Beast).

He and Kim are serious about parenthood. Peppa Pig was once allowed to be watched by the youngsters, but they stopped doing so due to Peppa's bad behavior. In an Instagram photo, he is wearing his kilt and a homemade Elsa tiara, which his girls described as a "skirt," proving that they have passed the Frozen period. He allows them to play the music from any program they enjoy in his car. "Gabby's Dollhouse is the source of the songs we are now listening to. And to be quite honest, I occasionally turn them on even when the kids aren't around."

Murray is completely distinct while still being so average in other aspects. He is surrounded by his family. Tennis, in contrast to team sports, pits one player against another, with the outcome decided point by point, often over hours. Does he feel lonely there?

He wants to minimize team sports when he states, "This is simply my feeling and I'm not downplaying team sports." "I'm confident that many team sports competitors are quite mentally tough individuals. But I enjoy that the outcome of an individual sport depends just on you. You'll probably lose if you play poorly. You will succeed if you play well. In contrast, even if you play very well on a team, you might still lose if your teammates play poorly. I appreciate that you can influence the result more directly.

However, being solitary is a difficult ability to master, and Murray found his early years as a professional to be quite challenging. You're not just doing it alone on the court, after all. Since you're the boss, in the end, he adds, "I suffered when I was younger. "You choose your trainer or physio, as well as your coaches. You also don't know who is excellent when you're 19, 20, or younger. Additionally, you are in charge of a group of workers who are often older than you. I was quite ignorant of all things, especially in terms of business. You can place your confidence in those who make promises to you but may only be thinking about themselves. And you're selecting a hire. Naomi Osaka, a four-time grand slam champion, is compelled to quit the French Open shortly after our conversation because she refused to speak to the press since it had a negative influence on her mental health. It makes me think of how stressed Murray was as a young man. Football teams have managers who face the heat from the media when they lose.

A baptism of fire occurred in his late teens. He faced David Nalbandian on Wimbledon's Center Court when he was 18 years old and lost in five sets (his legs cramped). This hitherto unknown Scottish adolescent, who had chosen tennis over football at the age of just 14, became well-known overnight.

He explains, "I went from playing in front of 10 or 15 people to playing on Centre Court in front of 15,000 people and millions of people on TV, getting pushed in front of TV cameras, being followed home, and having photographers outside my house. I was unsure of how to respond to it.

He now questions whether there is a way to prepare young people like him, whether sports regulating organizations should teach gifted adolescent athletes about finances, and train teams, how to face the press. He had to develop his public character on the job and for a very long time was known for being aggressive and defensive. He was the "moodiest, most wretched bastard," according to a joke made by Gabby Logan. But he wasn't; instead, he merely didn't like how the media depicted him.

In addition, he was emotionally erratic and single-minded, especially in court.

He claims that even now, he struggles to communicate his emotions to those who are close to him. When he was in his teens, he first noticed this: "I didn't know how to approach those talks. As a result, you find yourself saying nothing, which causes your frustration to increase. I still have trouble with it."

You seem pretty good to me, I say.

"Effectively, there are some persons and situations with whom I will converse well, and others with which I will not. This makes me seem like a lovely guy, which I'm not saying I am since I can be unkind in some circumstances. However, with my team, I've worked with a lot of my for a long time, and I don't want to frequently annoy them. So it's challenging for me to express my irritation to them.

He has intermittently collaborated with sports psychologists throughout his career, and when he was younger, "the question they constantly asked was, 'What would you tell your children?'" Which would you like for your children to do—something that makes them happy or something that leads to success? "Like most people, all I want is for my kids to be content. Therefore, it is preferable to work at something you love, even if you are not as successful at it as it is to work at something you detest, regardless of how successful you are. That's what I would say to my kids.

The success is fading, but there is no script for this. Will the joy also wane with time? What about the disappointment of accomplishing so much but never returning there? Mats Wilander, the 1980s world No. 1, expressed concern that Murray should deny young players wild cards; many armchair commentators share this concern.

Murray disputes this. One of the ways he has survived the last several years is because he has realized that life isn't fair. "If you live with the mindset that life isn't flawless, then you might be a little bit more prepared to handle it when something doesn't go as planned. In contrast, if your mindset is "Everything is wonderful all the time, I deserve everything," you'll undoubtedly experience disappointment frequently. He also has hope. He adored seeing Phil Mickelson, who is 50 years old and still plays golf, win the US PGA Championship in May. "I find that motivating." His eyes gleam.

Murray disputes this. One of the ways he has survived the last several years is because he has realized that life isn't fair. "If you live with the mindset that life isn't flawless, then you might be a little bit more prepared to handle it when something doesn't go as planned. In contrast, if your mindset is "Everything is wonderful all the time, I deserve everything," you'll undoubtedly experience disappointment frequently. He also has hope. He adored seeing Phil Mickelson, who is 50 years old and still plays golf, win the US PGA Championship in May. "I find that motivating." Do his eyes gleam? It's okay to criticize my performances and call me a dummy. But since I adore what I'm doing, I'll keep going till I can no longer.

Part One

THE MAKING OF ANDY MURRAY

The calm, energized person on display during consecutive triumphs in Melbourne this week may have been difficult for those who only see Andy Murray through the stressful two-week lens of Wimbledon fortnight to reconcile with the irritable Scot of popular imagination.

But the emergence of Murray mark 3, as his advisors, might call him, with new Adidas gear, without his ex-girlfriend, and with boxer Ricky Hatton joining his mother Judy and the rest of Team Murray to support him, is the most recent illustration of a change that experts predict will make him a future global sporting star.

Following Murray's signing to his 19 Entertainment stable last year, Simon Fuller, the Spice Girls mogul who rose to prominence in the entertainment industry through Pop Idol and David Beckham, and who is now Murray's manager, stated today that Murray's will to achieve set him apart.

"What I find most amazing about Andy, especially for someone so young, is his unwavering commitment to become the greatest. I have never encountered someone with such unwavering persistence and dedication as him. And Andy is a kind man," added Fuller. The extent to which he may advance in this sport has no bounds"

When he enters the Rod Laver arena on Sunday to face Roger Federer to become the first British man to win a singles championship in one of the four majors in 74 years, it might be the culmination of his transformation.

Even when he was making the SW19 set sulk into their G&Ts with his untidy mop, occasionally sullen demeanor, and infamous remark that he wanted anybody but England to win the 2006 World Cup, Murray was frequently towards the top of surveys among younger fans.

He was more appealing to a younger audience than many of his rivals and much beyond those who would traditionally be interested in tennis because of his sincerity and love of Twitter, boxing, martial arts, video games, practical jokes, and other activities.

The decisive moment on his route to his second Grand Slam final came when he chased down a lob and spun to deliver a jaw-dropping passing shot against Marin Cilic in the semifinals.

"Andy has improved a lot in the past year. He is incredibly confident and self-assured for his age.

He is a smart player, says Fuller, and his all-around game is developing at an extraordinary rate.

He has a strong sense of purpose and will stop at nothing to become the greatest golfer in the world.

When Fuller added Murray to his 19 stable last year, questions were raised. While many in the entertainment industry questioned whether Murray had the potential to become a worldwide celebrity, many in the sports world anticipated Murray to sign with an established international sports agency like IMG, which represents Federer and Tiger Woods and courted him aggressively.

The first thing he did was give his promotional packages more business sense. When Murray's advisors discovered that the clothes he was wearing were not readily accessible in stores, they were shocked.

With its extensive worldwide presence, Adidas will be an effective instrument in the rebranding process. It has a history in tennis, thanks to players like Stan Smith, Ivan Lendl, Steffi Graf, and Stefan Edberg, but it has slipped in popularity lately. Others are betting that Murray's triumph will start to inspire a new generation of British players, something that tens of millions of pounds in funding from the Lawn Tennis Association and constant hand-wringing have failed to do.

Becoming The British Sporting Hero

Just imagine, just for a second, what it must have felt like for Andy Murray.

And yet, serving for the title, you are down a breakpoint. Against the top player in the world and come back specialist Novak Djokovic. after possessing three match points.

I don't know about you, but I would be trembling so violently that I couldn't keep even one ball in play. Murray didn't serve underarm, which surprises me.

When I think back on it now, 48 hours later, it's still very chilling.

I believe it's crucial to relive those few great points on Centre Court at the All England Club to remind ourselves of what transpired and what Murray accomplished before we get carried away by fine clothes and talk of knighthoods.

In favor of Djokovic, The Serb appeared to be still sure of defeating the British favorite at that moment, grinning and gesturing to the audience as if to say, "We're going to be out here for another three hours and I'm going to have you in five."

However, Murray prevented Djokovic from capturing a second Wimbledon championship by winning that remarkable 10th game of the third set to show off his talent, tenacity, and drive to triumph.

The next 24 hours were crazy, to put it mildly. Murray conducted a series of television interviews right afterward, speaking with everyone from Sue Barker at the BBC to our colleagues at Wow Wow in Japan, who were just as thrilled if one of their own had won.

After checking to see whether someone was bringing him any sushi a half-hour later, he slouched into a chair in our little radio room and murmured that he didn't want to go since he was "so, so exhausted."

Sleep wouldn't come for some hours, though.

After more interviews, it was time for the Champions'Dinner at a posh Mayfair hotel.

In a dinner jacket and bow tie, standing with the trophy and making fun of Andrew Castle, he made an appearance at practically midnight.

His outstanding support staff proudly posed for the camera, and Ivan Lendl truly grinned.

I didn't catch him changing his smile. Lendl, who has played in two Wimbledon finals but has never won, has contributed significantly to Murray's success since joining Scot's team 18 months ago.

A similar example is the underrated effect of Murray's friend from his academy days in Spain, the soft-spoken Venezuelan Dani Vallverdu. Additionally, Murray's life is kept in order by Rob Stewart, physio Johan De Beer, and physical trainers Jez Green and Matt Little.

Andy Murray won the Wimbledon championship after defeating Novak Djokovic, the world's top player, 6-4 7-5 6-4.

Also keep Andy Ireland in your prayers; he reduced his work with Murray this year due to personal matters.

Murray would not be the person he is today without these men.

Murray slept for an hour and a half before a vehicle arrived outside his Surrey home to transport him back to Wimbledon for Monday morning's breakfast interviews.

It was exhausting, and some of the conversations may have been overly intrusive, but tennis got wonderful exposure.

Murray's victory at Wimbledon

Next, proceed to Downing Street for a meeting with Prime Minister David Cameron through a sponsored event in south London. Although Murray gave a sheepish wave to the photographers as he stood outside Number 10 with his hands in his pockets, he appeared to be the leader of the nation.

Perhaps we should have known when I look back to 2004 and the first time I encountered him, juggling tennis balls on both feet in a sports hall in Luxembourg. He listened to Tim Henman and Greg Rusedski throughout the Davis Cup weekend, taking notes.

Later that year, he cornered Sir Clive Woodward for information on England's 2003 World Cup victory at the BBC's Sports Personality of the Year awards event. Even though he was young and innocent, I knew he would become famous. He simply exuded such self-assurance.

His ATP main circuit debut occurred the following year, in 2005. His initial victories at Queens were followed by a three-set challenge to Grand Slam champion Thomas Johansson after his maiden encounter in Barcelona. Murray's performance distinguished him as one to watch even though he had a terrible cramp that forced him to leave the game.

At Wimbledon that summer, it was proven to be true. One of my favorite broadcasters, Tony Adamson, was dispatched by Radio 5 live to the old Court 2 to cover Murray's opening match against George Bastl.

I had no idea Tony would get a bit carried away on match point. Mark my words, Tony said. "This is a Wimbledon champion in the making!"

Following his triumph, Andy Murray spent a day with the Prime Minister.

When I was still very new to my position as tennis correspondent for 5 live, I recall lowering expectations by arguing that it was simply too early to predict Murray would win at the All England Club.

Tony, I apologize; we ought to have trusted you right then.

The first time I can recall feeling genuinely enthusiastic about watching Murray was when he defeated Radek Stepanek in straight sets in the second round.

On Court 1, Michael Stich and Tracy Austin, two previous Wimbledon champions, and I played in that match. Although they chuckled when I went beyond with my remarks, boy was they impressed.

I realized Murray was destined for the top 10 on that day.

It was great to learn more about the young Andy as 2005 went on. I felt it was excellent for tennis in Britain after the Henman years to have someone a little brasher, a little more vocal, even if I was already aware of his anti-establishment leanings.

He mimicked Jose Mourinho when he qualified for the US Open in August by putting his finger to his mouth in a celebratory motion.

There weren't many people in the little stand where we were sitting on Court 46 at the time. It felt like a odd thing to do.

People in Dunblane gathered outside to celebrate Andy Murray's triumph.

I pursued him into a hallway after he left the court. When I finally got up to him, he yelled into my microphone at people who said he wasn't physically fit enough. His next target was Wimbledon officials, who he said could have done more to let him enter the main draw at Flushing Meadows without having to qualify.

All of this just after winning a game...

Despite becoming extremely unwell on the court, he went on to defeat Andre Pavel in the first round of the US Open. He had just given a bold rejoinder, proving his endurance if there was any.

By this time, it was obvious that the media would have a significant impact on Murray's growth as a tennis player and a man.

He accused the assembled journalists of placing too much pressure on him when he was defeated in the first round of the Australian Open in 2006.

That May, we sat at a Hamburg café to watch the Champions League final. We chatted about the media and this bizarre, all-consuming world he had been thrust into as Barcelona defeated Arsenal on the big screen. He was and still is interesting company over burgers, fries, and lemonade.

Andy Murray talks to BBC Breakfast after historic Wimbledon win

The encounter with Rafael Nadal in Australia in 2007 is what changed my "top 10" forecast to "possible Grand Slam champion." The Spaniard prevailed in five sets, but Murray grabbed the initiative, modified his style of play to meet the challenge of competing against a huge celebrity, and came close to victory.

After the match, I became irritated with a former coworker who insisted Murray had lost despite making a tremendous effort.

Murray fluctuates between being a world-beater and a loser. Some people appear to believe that there is nothing in between.

Years in his early 20s were difficult for Murray as he was growing as a player and had a lot to learn off the court.

Early on, his trainers advised him that because the gym wasn't his favorite place to be, he needed to understand that the long hours will pay off in the end. There were also allegations that he disliked playing in the early morning hours because he valued his sleep too much. As a result, he dropped a few pointless matches, including some Grand Slam matches.

Again, he did not appreciate the critique, but after some thought, I'm sure he now sees its value.

He keeps getting better every day both as a person and a player.

And now he has won Wimbledon against intense public pressure and a shrinking number of detractors. It truly is a boy's account of perseverance, success, and inspiration.

DIVE DEEP

Originally from Scotland, Sir Andrew Barron Murray OBE is a British professional tennis player. He was born on May 15, 1987. The Association of Tennis Professionals (ATP) placed him as the top player in the world for 41 weeks, and he ended the year as the top player in 2016. Murray has won 14 Masters 1000 tournaments in addition to 46 ATP singles championships.

Murray, who was first trained by Judy, along with his older brother Jamie, traveled to Barcelona at the age of 15 to attend the Sánchez-Casal Academy. Around the time that Roger Federer and Rafael Nadal were the two top players in men's tennis, he started his professional career. When he debuted in the top 10 at the age of 19 in 2007, Murray enjoyed quick success on the ATP Tour. The Big Four, a group of players that dominated men's tennis in the 2010s, included Federer, Nadal, and Murray by the year 2010. Murray and Novak Djokovic later joined the Big Four. Murray originally had trouble facing the Big Four, dropping his first four championship matchups (three to Federer and one to Djokovic). By overcoming Djokovic to win the US Open in

2012, he achieved his big breakthrough, becoming the first British major singles champion since Virginia Wade in 1977 and the first man since Fred Perry in 1936. He defeated Federer to win the men's singles gold medal and the mixed doubles silver in the 2012 London Olympics one month earlier.

Murray made another six major finals from 2013 to 2016. At Wimbledon in 2013 and 2016, he prevailed in two of them. In 2016, Murray enjoyed the finest season of his career. Murray reached three major finals that year and won Wimbledon. In addition, he successfully defended his championship in the 2016 Summer Olympics in Rio, becoming the first player, male or female, to win two singles Olympic gold medals. Murray also rose to the top of the world for the first time this year after defeating Djokovic in the Tour Finals to secure the top spot for the whole year. Since 2016, he has battled several ailments, and in 2018 he dropped out of the top 100 owing to playing on tour so seldom. However, he has since steadily climbed back to the top 50.

Murray is an all-court player who is especially good in defense, serving and returning and building points. He is widely recognized as possessing one of the ATP Tour's best and most reliable two-handed backhands. For the first time since the early 20th century, Murray helped Great Britain become a dominant force in men's tennis, earning him the title of a national hero in that country. In 2015, he and his brother helped Great Britain win the Davis Cup. Murray has been public about being a feminist, and when he chose Amélie Mauresmo as his coach, he became just the second top-10 player in ATP Tour history to do so. Currently, he is alone among athletes who have beaten Novak Djokovic in a Wimbledon final.

Andy Murray was born in Glasgow, Scotland, the son of William Murray and Judy Murray (née Erskine). Roy Erskine, his maternal grandpa, played professional football in the late 1950s. Murray is a supporter of both Arsenal Football Club and Hibernian Football Club, one of the groups his grandpa played for.

When Murray was three years old, his mother Judy took him to the neighborhood tennis courts to play. At the age of five, he participated in his first competitive competition, and by the time he was eight, he was playing in the Central District Tennis League against adults. Jamie Murray, Andy Murray's older brother, competes professionally in tennis as a doubles player and has won many Grand Slam tournaments in both men's and mixed doubles.

Murray was raised in Dunblane and went to the local elementary school. Murray and his brother were there when Thomas Hamilton massacred 16 pupils and a teacher at Dunblane School in 1996 before turning the gun on himself. Murray sought refuge in a classroom. Although Murray is reluctant to discuss it in interviews because he claims he was too young to grasp what was going on, he claims in his memoirs Hitting Back that Hamilton ran a youth group he attended and that his mother offered Hamilton rides in her car. Later, Murray went to Dunblane High School.

When Murray's parents divorced when he was 10 years old, the boys moved live with their father while still receiving tennis coaching from their mother. He thinks the effect this had on him may be what spurs his competitive nature. He was invited to train with Rangers Football Club at their School of Excellence when he was 15 but turned it down to concentrate on his tennis career. He subsequently decided to go to Barcelona, Spain. He attended the

Schiller International School there and trained under Pato Alvarez's coaching on the clay courts at the Sanchez-Casal Academy. Murray called this period "a significant sacrifice." His 18-month stay there required his parents to come up with £40,000 in funding. He received training from former No. 1 doubles player in the world Emilio Sánchez in Spain.

Murray was born with a bipartite patella, a condition in which the kneecap does not fuse in early infancy but instead persists as two distinct bones. He was not identified with this problem, however, until he was 16 years old. Due to the agony the ailment causes, he has been spotted cradling his knee and has withdrawn from events as a result.

Murray paid £1.8 million in February 2013 to purchase the Cromlix House hotel close to Dunblane. Although it subsequently stopped operating, brother Jamie held his wedding there in 2010. In April 2014, the location reopened as a 15-room, five-star hotel. In acknowledgment of his contributions to tennis, Murray earned an honorary doctorate from the University of Stirling later that month as well as the freedom of Stirling.

In 2005, Murray started dating Kim Sears, the child of former player and current coach Nigel Sears. They announced their engagement in November 2014, and on April 11, 2015, they were married at Dunblane Cathedral in his hometown of Glasgow, with the celebration taking place at his Cromlix House hotel. The family, which consists of their son and three daughters—the youngest of whom was born in March 2021—moved from Oxshott, Surrey, to the adjacent town of Leatherhead in 2022. The couple had previously resided in Oxshott.

He has frequently shown his support for female athletes and coaches and describes himself as a feminist. He also speaks out in favor of same-sex marriage and LGBT rights. He also expressed solidarity for the Black Lives Matter movement in June 2020 by taking a knee with other athletes at the Schroders Battle of the Brits. He declared he was "totally supportive" of Naomi Osaka's choice to skip her semi-final match at the Western & Southern Open in the aftermath of Jacob Blake's shooting in Wisconsin just before the 2020 US Open. Osaka finally decided to play the match.

Murray has used the crowdsourcing website Seeds to invest in up to 30 UK companies.

Before traveling to Melbourne for the Australian Open in January 2021, Murray tested positive for COVID-19 and was placed in quarantine and isolation at home, ultimately missing the competition.

Following the birth of their fourth child, Murray decided to leave the Dubai Duty Free Tennis Championships in March 2021. In October 2021, Murray traveled to California to participate in the Indian Wells Tennis Championships. After practicing, he claimed that his trainers—but more significantly, his wedding ring—had been taken from underneath his car in the hotel parking lot. His sneakers and wedding ring were returned to him in time for his first competitive tennis match in four years at Indian Wells after numerous pleas on social media and in the media.

Junior Career

Murray's tennis coach from age 11 to age 17 Leon Smith characterized him as "unbelievably competitive," and Murray says his talent stems from the drive he developed after losing to his elder brother Jamie. Murray won his age division in the Orange Bowl, a famous competition for young athletes, in 1999 when he was 12 years old. In the 70-year history of the Junior Orange Bowl tournament, only nine tennis players—including Jimmy Connors, Jennifer Capriati, and Monica Seles—have won it twice. He did so when he was 14 years old.

Murray began competing in Challenger and Futures events in July 2003. He advanced to the Manchester Challenger quarterfinals in his debut competition. Murray earned his first senior championship in September by winning the Glasgow Futures competition. He also advanced to the Edinburgh Futures competition's semifinals.

Murray Missed The First Six Months Of 2004 Due To A Knee Ailment.

Murray competed in a Challenger tournament in Nottingham in July 2004. In the second round, he was defeated by future Grand Slam finalist Jo-

Wilfried Tsonga. Murray later won Futures competitions in Xativa and Rome.

He won the Junior US Open in September 2004 and was chosen for the Davis Cup World Group play-off match against Austria later that month, however, he was not chosen to participate. He was named the BBC Young Sports Personality of the Year later that year.

Murray rose to No. 6 in the world as a junior in 2003. (and No. 8 in doubles). He came in at No. 2 in the world in the combined rankings that were introduced in 2004.

Professional Career

2005: Turning professional

Murray started the year 2005 rated No. 407, but he had to take three months off after hurting his back while traveling in South America in January.

He played in the Davis Cup as the country's youngest player in March. After turning pro in April, Murray received a wild card entrance to the Open SEAT, a clay-court competition in Barcelona. There, he was defeated by Jan Hernych in three sets. Murray bitterly split from Pato Alvarez as his coach in April, blaming him for having a bad attitude. Murray later advanced to the boys' French Open semifinals, when he was defeated by Marin Ili in straight sets.

Mark Petchey agreed to mentor Murray for four weeks until Wimbledon ended, but the job eventually turned into a full-time one. Murray, who was given a wild card to Queen's, beat Santiago Ventura in straight sets to advance and win his maiden ATP match. After defeating Taylor Dent in the second round, he played Thomas Johansson in the third round, losing in three sets as a result of cramps and an ankle injury. Murray was given a wild card into Wimbledon as a result of his success at Queen's. Murray, who entered Wimbledon's men's singles competition at No. 312, became the first Scot in the Open Era to go to the third round. Murray fell to 2002 Wimbledon finalist David Nalbandian in the third round after leading two sets to one because of cramps and exhaustion.

Murray won Challenger competitions on the hard courts at Aptos and Binghamton, New York after Wimbledon. He subsequently competed in his first Master's competition in Cincinnati, where he defeated Taylor Dent before falling to the No. 4 seed, Marat Safin, in three sets. In the US Open's first round, Murray faced Andrei Pavel as a wild card entrant, and he came back from being down two sets to one to win his first five-set match. He was defeated by Arnaud Clément in a second-round matchup in five sets, though. Murray was chosen once more to compete against Switzerland in the

Davis Cup. He was chosen for the initial singles match, losing to Stanislas Wawrinka in straight sets. At the Thailand Open, Murray competed in his first ATP final against No. 1 Roger Federer. Murray was defeated in three sets.

At the Basel Swiss Indoors, Murray defeated Tim Henman in their first encounter and went on to the quarterfinals.

Murray led Scotland in the inaugural Aberdeen Cup match against Greg Rusedski's England in November.

Murray only ever faced Rusedski in an exhibition match; they never crossed paths on the Tour. Murray won the second match, but Rusedski had won the previous one. Additionally, Andy Murray and his brother Jamie Murray participated in doubles for the first time as seniors. England was trounced 412–2 by Scotland. He finished the year in 64th place, and in 2005, BBC Scotland named him Sports Personality of the Year.

2006: First ATP title and British No. 1

Murray made his full-circuit debut in 2006, parted ways with Mark Petchey as his coach, and teamed up with Brad Gilbert.

For the first time, Murray upset Andy Roddick in the SAP Open in San Jose in February. Murray eventually defeated No. 11 Lleyton Hewitt to win the championship. Murray eventually overtook Tim Henman as the British No. 1 and ended his seven-year reign. Tim Henman was now ranked 49th, Murray was ranked 42nd, and Greg Rusedski was ranked 43rd. On May 15, 1994, Rusedski once again held the title of British No. 1 for eight weeks.

Murray lost to Juan Ignacio Chela of Argentina in straight sets in the opening round of the Australian

71

Open. lost in five sets to Gael Monfils at the French Open. At Wimbledon (when he defeated third seed Andy Roddick in the third round) and the US Open, Murray did go to the fourth round for the first time.

In Davis Cup matches against Serbia, Israel, and Ukraine, Murray participated. Before losing the doubles match and Britain losing their tie with Serbia, Murray didn't play in the early singles matches. Murray won his rubber during the encounter with Israel but lost the doubles. Before the reverse singles, Murray withdrew due to a neck injury, and Britain lost the match.

Murray defeated Ukraine by winning both of his singles rubbers, but he fell short in the doubles as Britain took the match.

In Miami, Monte Carlo, and Rome at the Masters, Murray was defeated in the opening round. In the second round of the competitions in Indian Wells and Hamburg, Murray was eliminated. At the Rogers Cup in Toronto, Murray competed in his maiden Master's semifinal but lost to Richard Gasquet.

In Cincinnati, Andy Murray ended Roger Federer's 55-match winning run on hard courts and became just one of two players, along with Rafael Nadal, to do it in 2006.

He fell to Andy Roddick in the next two rounds, although he made his maiden appearance in the top 20. With losses to Novak Djokovic and Dominik Hrbat, Murray ended his season in the last 16 stages of the two last Masters tournaments in Madrid and Paris. Murray competed in the Legg Mason Tennis Classic final. In Bangkok, he competed in doubles alongside his brother, and the two made it to the final. Murray said that his bones hadn't fully matured, causing him to experience cramping and back issues, after the French Open, when he was once more injured.

The Aberdeen Cup was played for the second time in November, with Murray serving as Scotland's captain and Greg Rusedski as England's. Scots prevailed 612-1.

2007: Ascending to the top 10

Murray advanced to the fourth round of the Australian Open before falling to No. 2 Rafael Nadal in a five-set encounter.

After competing in the Miami Masters and making it to the semifinals, Murray rose to the No. 10 spot on April 16.

During his encounter in the German Open's first round at Hamburg, the British No. 1 suffered tendon damage. When Murray's wrist tendons were severed by a forehand from the back of the court when he was up 5-1, he missed Wimbledon and was sidelined from 15 May to 7 August. Murray reached No. 8 during this time of relaxation, but by August 7 he had fallen to No. 14.

At the US Open, Murray lost in the third round. Murray advanced to the Indian Wells and Miami semifinals of the Master's events. Murray lost in the first round in Rome and Cincinnati but lost in the second round in Canada. Murray was eliminated from the final two masters championships in the third round in Madrid and the quarterfinals in Paris. Murray won championships in St. Petersburg and San Jose. While completing the season ranked 11th in the world, he also made it to the finals of events in Doha and Metz.

In November, Murray parted ways with his coach Brad Gilbert and hired a group of specialists in addition to Miles Maclagan as his primary trainer.

2008: First major final and Masters titles

Murray at the 2008 US Open

In 2008, Murray lost to eventual runner-up Jo-Wilfried Tsonga in the first round of the Australian Open and to Nicolás Almagro in the third round of the French Open. Before competing in his maiden US Open final, Murray advanced to the quarterfinals at Wimbledon, his first Grand Slam event. Murray defeated Nadal for the first time at the New York event. With his victory, he became the first British player to reach a major final since Greg Rusedski in 1997. Murray lost to Federer in straight sets in his maiden Grand Slam final. Murray lost to Taiwan's No. 77 Yen-Hsun Lu in straight sets in the first round of the singles competition at the Beijing Olympics, one of the worst losses of his professional career. Despite an Olympic gold medal and a head-to-head victory in the meantime, that humiliating loss was still fresh in his memory five years later, when he faced the same opponent (now ranked No. 75) in the Wimbledon second round.

Murray was eliminated from the Master's competitions in the fourth round in Indian Wells and the opening round in Miami. In the clay Masters, Murray advanced to the third round in Rome and both Monte Carlo and Hamburg. Murray reached the semifinals of Toronto on the American hard court circuit before taking home his first Masters trophy in Cincinnati.

Before falling short in the quarterfinals of Paris, he added another shield to his collection in Madrid. Murray, who is now ranked No. 4 in the world, achieved his first Masters Cup qualification. Despite playing well enough to upset an ailing Federer, he was defeated by Davydenko in the semifinals. In 2008, Murray was rated No. 4.

Murray also prevailed in competitions held in Doha, Marseille, and St. Petersburg.

2009: Ascent to world No. 2 and two Masters titles

At the Qatar Open in Doha, Murray successfully defended his championship by defeating Andy Roddick in straight sets to kick off the 2009 season. Murray lost to Fernando Verdasco in the fourth round of the Australian Open. Murray defeated No. 1 Nadal in three sets to win his eleventh career championship in Rotterdam. The infection that had previously afflicted Murray at the Australian Open flared up again when he traveled to Dubai, forcing him to withdraw before the quarterfinals. Murray missed a Davis Cup game in Glasgow as a result of sickness. Then, Murray lost to Nadal in the Indian Wells final but defeated Djokovic a week later to win another masters championship in Miami.

Before the French Open, Murray defeated No. 9 Nikolay Davydenko in the Monte Carlo Masters, becoming the first top-ten player to be defeated on clay. Despite this victory, Murray fell to Nadal in the semi-finals. Murray was defeated by qualifier Juan Mónaco in round two of the Rome Masters, and he lost to Juan Martin del Potro in the quarterfinals of the Madrid Masters. When he attained the No. 3 spot on May 11, 2009, Murray became the first British man to hold that position in the Open Era. Murray advanced to the French Open quarterfinals but lost to Fernando González in four sets.

Murray became the first British champion of the competition since 1938 and won a championship for the first time on the grass at Queen's. James Blake, an American, was beaten by Murray in the final. Murray's Wimbledon match in the fourth round versus Stanislas Wawrinka was the first to be played fully under the retractable roof. This made it possible for it to be the then-latest concluding match at Wimbledon, a record he would subsequently break three years later in a match against Marcos Baghdatis in the second round. However, Andy Roddick defeated Murray in a close semifinal match.

In Montreal, Murray made a comeback and defeated del Potro in three sets to win the championship.

He passed Nadal in the rankings after this triumph, and he kept that spot until the US Open began. Following his victory in the Masters, Murray competed in the Cincinnati Masters, where he was defeated by Federer. Due to a wrist injury, Murray was unable to compete at the US Open and lost to Ili in straight sets. Murray defeated Poland in the Davis Cup doubles match, winning both of his singles sets, but then suffered a wrist injury that caused him to miss six weeks of play.

Murray won in Valencia in November but lost in the second round of the Paris Masters. Murray failed to get past the round of 16 at the World Tour Finals in London to cap the campaign. For the second year in a row, he finished the year in fourth place.

2010: Hopman Cup and Australian Open finals

At the Hopman Cup, Murray and Laura Robson represented Great Britain. The duo advanced to the championship game, where Spain defeated them. Murray defeated Nadal and "ili" in the Australian Open before falling to Roger Federer in the championship match.

Murray said in his acceptance speech after finishing in second place at the 2010 Australian Open, "I can weep like Roger, it's just a bad I can't play like him."

Murray lost to Robin Söderling in straight sets in the quarterfinals of the BNP Paribas Open in Indian Wells. After losing his opening match of the 2010 Sony Ericsson Open to Mardy Fish, Murray claimed that his focus hadn't been entirely on the game of tennis. Murray lost his opening match in the Monte-Carlo Rolex Masters, this time to Philipp Kohlschreiber. He and Ross Hutchins competed in the doubles event, but they fell short of the Bryan Brothers in the champions tie-breaker. In both the Rome Masters and the Madrid Masters, Murray advanced to the third round before falling to David Ferrer both times.

Murray reached his second Grand Slam Final in Australia

Following an exhibition match, Murray began the French Open with three grueling victories before falling to Tomá Berdych in straight sets in the fourth round. Murray advanced to the third round in London, where he faced Mardy Fish. The match was abandoned due to poor lighting when it was 3-3 in the fourth set and Murray had the momentum (he had recently recovered from a 3-0 deficit). Murray was furious. Returning the next day, Murray lost to the eventual winner in a tie-breaker for the second time this year. Murray advanced to the Wimbledon semifinals before falling to Nadal in straight sets. After parting ways with his coach Maclagan on July 27, 2010, Murray hired Lex Corretja in his place.

The 2010 Farmers Classic marked the beginning of the US hard-court season. Murray advanced to the final but fell to Sam Querrey in three sets. In their previous five encounters, this was his first defeat to Querrey. Since Andre Agassi in 1995, Murray is the only player in Canada to successfully defend the Canadian Masters. Murray ended his eight-month championship drought by sweeping Nadal and then Federer in straight sets. In a quarterfinal encounter against Fish at the Cincinnati Masters, Murray first complained about the pace of the court before complaining that the organizers would not schedule the match for a later time. Murray prevailed in a tiebreaker to take the opening set despite feeling sick in 33 °C of heat in the shadow.

The 2010 Farmers Classic marked the beginning of the US hard-court season. Murray advanced to the final but fell to Sam Querrey in three sets. In their previous five encounters, this was his first defeat to Querrey. Since Andre Agassi in 1995, Murray is the only player in Canada to successfully defend the

Canadian Masters. Murray ended his eight-month championship drought by sweeping Nadal and then Federer in straight sets. In a quarterfinal encounter against Fish at the Cincinnati Masters, Murray first grumbled about the pace of the court before complaining that the organizers would not schedule the match for later in the day. Murray prevailed in a tiebreaker to take the opening set despite feeling sick in 33 °C of heat in the shadow.

However, Murray beat Mahesh Bhupathi and Max Mirnyi in the doubles final with his brother Jamie Murray. The triumph was Murray's first doubles championship and his second appearance in a final alongside his brother.

Murray lost to Gael Monfils in three sets at the BNP Paribas Masters quarterfinals.

The combination of his elimination and Söderling winning the match caused Murray to drop from No. 4 to No. 5 in the rankings.

In round-robin play at the Tour Finals in London, Murray finished with a 2-1 record before playing Nadal in the semifinal. They fought for more than three hours before Murray lost to the Spaniard in a tiebreaker in the final set, ending his season. For the third year in a row, he finished the year in fourth place.

2011: Consistency in slams and two more Masters

Despite winning both of his singles matches, Murray and Laura Robson lost the 2011 Hopman Cup round-robin stage, dropping all three of their ties. Then Murray joined other famous athletes like Federer, Nadal, and Djokovic in the Rally for Relief event to support the Queensland flood victims.

Jamie Murray and Murray at the 2011 Japan Open

Murray, who was the fifth seed at the 2011 Australian Open, lost in straight sets against Novak Djokovic, a past winner. He lost to Marcos Baghdatis in Rotterdam's opening round. With his brother Jamie, Murray advanced to the doubles competition semifinals. In the opening stages of the Masters Series competitions in Indian Wells and Miami, Murray was defeated by qualifiers; as a result, he and his coach, Lex Corretja, parted ways.

At the Monte-Carlo Rolex Masters, Murray found his form again but fell to Nadal in the semifinals.

Before the game, Murray hurt his elbow, and as a result, he withdrew from the 2011 Barcelona Open Banco Sabadell. The Mutua Madrilea Madrid Open saw Murray lose in the third round, but he advanced to the semi-finals of the Rome Masters before falling to Novak Djokovic.

Murray won two challenging opening sets at the French Open before falling to Rafael Nadal in his maiden semi-final at Roland Garros.

Murray won the second Queen's Club championship by defeating Jo-Wilfried Tsonga. Despite winning the opening set at Wimbledon, Murray was defeated by Nadal in the semi-final. Murray steered the British team to win the Davis Cup match between the United Kingdom and Luxembourg. Murray, the reigning two-time Rogers Cup winner, was defeated by Kevin Anderson of South Africa in the second round. But after Novak Djokovic withdrew due to injury the next week, he took home the 2011 Western & Southern Open title. At the 2011 US Open, Murray overcame a two-set deficit to defeat Robin Haase in five sets, but he fell to Rafael Nadal in the semifinals in four.

For the first time in his professional career, Andy finished in the quarterfinals or higher in all four slams in a single year.

Murray comfortably won the 250-class Thailand Open, and the following week, at the Rakuten Japan Open Tennis Championships, he claimed his third victory in as many competitions. Rafael Nadal was his opponent in the championship match, and he defeated him in three sets for the first time this year. Then Murray and his brother Jamie Murray won the doubles match, making Murray the first player in the 2011 season to win both the singles and doubles championships at the same tournament. Murray then defeated David Ferrer in straight sets in the championship match to successfully defend his Shanghai Masters title.

Murray suffered a groin strain after losing to David Ferrer in straight sets at the ATP World Tour Finals, and he withdrew from the competition. For the fourth year running, Murray finished the year ranked #4, trailing Djokovic, Nadal, and Federer.

2012: Olympic Gold, US Open champion, and Wimbledon runner-up

Murray's new full-time coach, Ivan Lendl, helped him start the season by participating in the 2012 Brisbane International. He overcame a sluggish start in his first two sets to defeat Alexandr Dolgopolov in the final and won his 22nd championship. He fell short in a close encounter against the second seeds in doubles, Jürgen Melzer and Philipp Petzschner, in the quarterfinals. After competing in an exhibition match, Murray advanced to the 2012 Australian Open semifinals before falling to Djokovic in a match that lasted four hours and 50 minutes.

Murray overcame Djokovic in the semi-finals of the Dubai Duty-Free Tennis Championships, but Roger Federer won the match. Murray lost to Djokovic in the Miami Masters final after suffering an early loss in the BNP Paribas Open. Following those defeats, Murray lost in the third round of the Italian Open, the Monte Carlo Masters quarterfinals, and the Barcelona Open. Murray overcame spasms the whole French Open, but David Ferrer defeated him in the quarterfinals.

Murray was defeated by No. 65 Nicolas Mahut in the first round of the Queen's Club Championships.

When Murray defeated Marcos Baghdatis in four sets at Wimbledon, the play was finished at 23:02

BST, breaking the previous record for the championships. The 2018 Wimbledon men's singles semifinals, which saw play end at 23:03 BST, broke the previous record.

Since Bunny Austin in 1938, Murray became the first male British player to reach the Wimbledon final after defeating Jo-Wilfried Tsonga in the semi-final in four sets. He met Federer in the championship match, but after winning the opening set, he was defeated in four sets.

Within a few weeks, Murray was back at Wimbledon, this time to take part in the singles, doubles, and mixed doubles competitions at the London 2012 Summer Olympics. He lost in the opening round of the doubles competition with his brother Jamie Murray to Austria (Jürgen Melzer and Alexander Peya) in three sets. Laura Robson and Murray played in the mixed doubles. They advanced to the championship match, but they were defeated in three sets by the top-seeded Belarusians, Victoria Azarenka, and Max Mirnyi, and had to settle for the silver medal. In singles, Murray only dropped one set en route to the finals, where he faced Federer and won in straight sets with just seven games lost. Murray became only the seventh man in the open era to win two medals at the same Olympic Games by taking home the gold medal. He was also the first British man to win the tennis Olympic singles gold medal since Josiah Ritchie in 1908. Due to a knee injury, Murray withdrew from the Rogers Cup early, and in the Cincinnati Masters, unseeded Jérémy Chardy defeated him in straight sets.

Murray at the US Open in 2012, where he won his maiden major championship.

After that, he participated in the US Open, the season's last major.

He defeated Alex Bogomolov and Ivan Dodig in straight sets in his first two rounds before taking on Feliciano Lopez in a challenging four-set match that required Murray to prevail in three tiebreakers.

He overcame Canadian Milos Raonic in the fourth round in straight sets and then had to rally to beat Marin Ili in the quarterfinals after falling by a set and two breaks.

He overcame Tomas Berdych in the semi-finals in a hard-fought encounter that lasted almost four hours to advance to his second straight Grand Slam final.

Murray became the first British man to win a Grand Slam final since Fred Perry in 1936 after defeating Djokovic in five sets, and since Harold Mahony in 1896, the only Scottish-born athlete to triumph in a Grand Slam final. Murray's victory would also break several records: the match featured the longest tiebreak in US Open final history at 12-10 in the first set, and he became the first person to ever win both the US Open and an Olympic gold medal in the same year, and the match was tied with the 1988 US Open final (in which Murray's coach Lendl participated) for the lengthiest match in the history of the competition. In the championship match, Murray defeated Djokovic to win the 100th Grand Slam match of his career. Many commentators and contemporary players, notably Novak Djokovic, referred to Murray's victory as putting him among the "Big Four."

Murray entered the Rakuten Japan Open as the defending champion and advanced to the semifinals in his first competition following the US Open. Milos Raonic defeated him in a competitive three-set encounter. He and his brother Jamie were the defending doubles champions. However, they were eliminated in the quarterfinals by Leander Paes and

Radek Tpánek, the top seeds. After gaining a bye into round two at the last Masters 1000 tournament of the year in Shanghai, Murray was scheduled to play Florian Mayer in his opening round. Due to Mayer's withdrawal due to injury, Murray received a walkover into round three. In the third round, he defeated Alexandr Dolgopolov; in the quarterfinal, he defeated Radek Tpánek in three sets. Murray next played Roger Federer in the semifinals, which he won in straight sets to advance to his third straight Shanghai final versus Djokovic and a rematch with Federer. Murray's 12-0 winning record in the competition came to an end when he lost in three sets after wasting five match opportunities. Murray concluded the year at No. 3 after spending the previous four years at No. 4 due to Nadal's withdrawal from the Paris Masters and the year-end tournaments. Murray has never placed higher than No. 4 in the year-end rankings before. Murray placed third overall in the BBC Sports

Personality of the Year, ahead of Mo Farah. At the Laureus World Sports Awards, Murray was named the World Breakthrough of the Year.

In the 2013 New Year's Honours, Murray received the OBE designation for his contributions to tennis.

Wimbledon winner in 2013 underwent back surgery

Murray won the Brisbane International again in 2013 and defeated Grigor Dimitrov in the championship match in straight sets.

He had a strong start at the 2013 Australian Open by defeating Dutchman Robin Haase in straight sets while attempting to win his second major in a row.

Following this, he defeated Joo Sousa, practice partner Riardas Berankis, and French No. 14 seed Gilles Simon in straight sets.

He defeated Jérémy Chardy in the quarterfinals in straight sets to get to a match against Roger Federer in the semifinals. Murray finally won in five sets after trading sets, becoming the first player to defeat Federer in a Grand Slam competition. With this triumph, Federer, Nadal, Djokovic, and Murray had all defeated the other three major champions, making them the ATP's most powerful foursome of the previous four years. With this triumph, Murray will play in his second consecutive match versus Djokovic and his third straight major final. Murray won the opening set in a tiebreaker before losing in the next four sets. Murray lost in this year's Australian Open final, making Stefan Edberg the only other player to have finished third three times in the Open Era.

Murray was defeated by Juan Martin del Potro in the quarterfinals of the BNP Paribas Open at Indian Wells in three sets. Murray won his first four matches in the Miami Masters without dropping a set, and after defeating Richard Gasquet in the semifinals, he took on David Ferrer in the championship match. Murray won the match in a third-set tiebreaker after dropping the first set and facing match point in the decider at 5-6 to win his second Miami Masters title and overtake Roger Federer in the rankings. This marks the end of a nearly ten-year stretch in which either Federer or Rafael Nadal held the top two spots.

After losing to Stanislas Wawrinka in the Monte-Carlo third round, Murray momentarily dropped to No. 3, but he quickly rose back to No. 2 as a result of Federer's failure to successfully defend his title at the Mutua Madrid Open. Later, Murray was defeated in straight sets by Tomas Berdych in the quarterfinals.

On his 26th birthday, Murray played Marcel Granollers in the second round of the Rome

Masters before retiring due to a hip ailment. After taking the second set on a tiebreak, Murray rallied back to tie the match at one set each. Murray now had just eleven days to be healthy in time for the start of the French Open. After the game, Murray spoke during a news conference and said, "As it is, I'd be shocked beyond belief if I was performing in Paris. I must develop a strategy for my actions. I'll have a conversation with the men tonight, organize the following three days, and then decide on Paris after the next five days." Later, he would claim a back injury as the reason for pulling out of Roland Garros. Murray returned in the 2013 Aegon Championships, where he was the top seed, after missing four weeks due to injury. Next a first-day weather delay, Murray was forced to play Nicolas Mahut in the second round and Marinko Matosevic in the following round on the same day. Murray won both matches in straight sets. After defeating Benjamin Becker in the quarterfinals, Murray faced

Jo-Wilfried Tsonga in the semifinals, his first top-ten opponent since losing to Tomá Berdych in Madrid. After losing the opening set against the Frenchman, Murray gradually improved and won in three sets to go to his third straight grass court final against Marin Ili of Croatia. He once more overcame a deficit to defeat ili in three sets and win his third crown at Queen's Club.

Before Wimbledon, Murray had not dropped a set on grass since the championship match of the previous season and was on an 11-match winning run. Murray defeated Yen-Hsun Lu and Benjamin Becker in straight sets in the first two rounds, respectively. After the unexpected early exits of Roger Federer and Rafael Nadal, Murray faced 32nd seed Tommy Robredo in the third round. Despite a comeback on the tour over the past year, Murray defeated the Spaniard in straight sets to advance to a match with Mikhail Youzhny, the highest seed left in Murray's half. Murray overcame a comeback in the second set to win in straight sets and advance to his eighth straight Grand Slam quarterfinal, where he would meet Fernando Verdasco, a left-handed player who had not met Murray since the 2012 US Open. Murray overcame a two-set deficit for the seventh time in his career to win in five sets, setting up a semifinal matchup with Jerzy Janowicz, the 24th seed and the Polish player who defeated Murray in their first meeting. Murray committed a double fault, which allowed Janowicz to win the first set in a tiebreak after he was unable to break his serve. However, Murray was able to step up his game and win the following three sets, advancing to his second straight Wimbledon final and third straight major final against Novak Djokovic.

The British men's singles champion since Fred Perry in 1936, Murray defeated Djokovic in a straight sets match that lasted more than three hours to become the first Scot of either sex to win a Wimbledon singles title since Harold Mahony in 1896, and he extended his winning streak on grass to 18 matches. Despite the Serb being the favorite to win the title throughout the Championships.

For the first time, Murray at the US Open entered a Grand Slam event as the defending champion and got off to a fast start by defeating Michal Llodra in straight sets. He followed this up by defeating Denis Istomin, Leonardo Mayer, and Florian Mayer to advance to the quarterfinals at a major for the eleventh consecutive match. Murray lost in straight sets against Swiss player Stanislas Wawrinka in the round of 8, snapping his string of four straight major final appearances. Murray joined the Great Britain Davis Cup squad for their World Group Play-off match on clay against Croatia after his dismal run of results on hard courts, and he participated in two singles and the doubles rubbers. In the doubles match, Murray and Colin Fleming defeated Croatia's top-ranked players Ivan Dodig and Mate Pavi to take a 2-1 lead in the series after overcoming 16-year-old Borna "ori" in straight sets. Murray then defeated Dodig in straight sets to clinch Britain's return to the World Group.

Murray's season was cut short after the Davis Cup when he decided to have surgery to address the lower back issues that had plagued him since the start of the previous season. Murray decided that surgery was the best long-term solution after being forced to retire from the French Open in May due to an ailment that flared up again at the US Open and again during the Davis Cup World Group Play-offs. Murray won the 2013 BBC Sports Personality of the Year award following the 2013 season, having been a strong favorite since before the candidates were revealed.

2014: 30th career title and out of the top 10

Murray's campaign got underway in Doha at the Qatar Open. He overcame No. 40, Florian Mayer, in three sets in the second round despite being a set and a break up three games into the second set. In the first round, he defeated Mousa Shanan Zayed in straight sets in 37 minutes without conceding a single game. At the 2014 AAMI Classic in Kooyong, he then played a warm-up match against No. 43 Lleyton Hewitt, losing in two tight tiebreaks.

He then traveled to Melbourne for the 2014 Australian Open, where he was drawn against Japanese player Go Soeda at No. 112. Murray got off to a solid start despite concerns that he was not match-fit, dismissing the Japanese number 2 in under 90 minutes while losing just 5 games overall. The next two opponents he defeated in straight sets were Feliciano Lopez and Vincent Millot. In the fourth round, Murray lost his first set of the competition before defeating Stephane Robert in four sets to set up a quarterfinal matchup with longtime rival Roger Federer. Despite surviving two match chances to win the third set, he ultimately lost in four sets, snapping a run of four straight semi-final appearances at the Australian Open. Murray lost before the championship match and dropped to No. 6, missing the top five for the first time since 2008.

After that, he traveled to America to battle Great Britain in the first round of the Davis Cup World Group, who entered the match as underdogs. Murray helped Britain advance to their first Davis Cup quarterfinal since 1986 by winning both of his matches against Donald Young and Sam Querrey, respectively. Following a late wild card, Murray competed in the Rotterdam Open, where he was defeated in the quarterfinals by Marin Ili in straight sets. In his next match, the Mexican Open in Acapulco, he lost to Grigor Dimitrov in the semifinals in a dramatic three-set match that took two tiebreakers to decide the last two sets.

At Indian Wells, Murray battled in his first two matches against Luká Rosol and Ji Vessel, but he won both of them in hard-fought three-set battles to advance to a match against Canadian Milos Raonic in the fourth round, which he ultimately lost in three sets. Murray was unable to persuade anyone to join him on the court, so Murray offered to play with the 2012 Wimbledon Doubles winner. Murray and Marry defeated Gal Monfils and Juan Mónaco in their first competitive match together, but they fell to the No. 2 seeds Alexander Peya and Bruno Soares in the second round.

Ivan Lendl, who had received many accolades for assisting Murray in realizing his dream of collecting Grand Slam championships, and Murray parted ways in March. Murray won against Matthew Ebden, Feliciano López, and Jo Wilfried Tsonga at the 2014 Miami Masters before falling to Djokovic in the quarterfinals. He defeated Andreas Seppi in the opening round of the Davis Cup quarterfinal match against Italy before teaming up with Colin Fleming to win the doubles set. In his last singles encounter, Murray was defeated in straight sets by Fabio Fognini, who had only previously defeated one top 10 players on clay, Nikolay Davydenko, back in 2009. This forced Great Britain to play the decisive final rubber. However, James Ward, a fellow countryman, lost to Andreas Seppi in this match in straight sets, disqualifying Murray and Great Britain from the Davis Cup.

Then Murray participated in the Madrid Open, where he dedicated his opening victory over Nicolas Almagro to former star Elena Baltacha.

After that, he was defeated by qualifier Santiago Giraldo in the next round. After that, Murray advanced to the quarterfinals of the Rome Masters, where he fell to Rafael Nadal in a close encounter after leading by a break in the last set. In the last set of the French Open, Murray edged out the 28th seed Philipp Kohlschreiber 12-10 after defeating Andrey Golubev and Marinko Matosevic. Murray has never advanced past 7-5 in a decisive set before. Following this, he defeated Fernando Verdasco in straight sets, and in the quarterfinals, he defeated Frenchman Gal Monfils in five sets, moving Murray up to No. 5 and matching his greatest French Open performance by making it to the semifinals. However, he went on to lose in straight sets against Nadal, winning just 6 games overall. In a "historic decision," Murray hired Amélie Mauresmo as his coach after losing to Rafael Nadal in the 2014 French Open semifinals. This became

Mauresmo the first woman to train a top-ranked male tennis player.

Murray was placed third in the 2014 Wimbledon Championship after successful grass court seasons in 2012 and 2013, trailing Novak Djokovic and Rafael Nadal, who was seeded first and second, respectively. To begin his title defense, he defeated Bla Rola and David Goffin in straight sets with the latter losing just two games. In straight sets, Murray defeated the 27th and 20th seeds, Roberto Bautista Agut and Kevin Anderson, to advance to his sixth consecutive Wimbledon quarterfinal. Then, Murray's defense came to an end as Grigor Dimitrov defeated him in straight sets to snap his 17-match winning streak on Wimbledon's grass (which also includes the 2012 Olympics). This was Murray's first semi-final exit since 2008. Murray slid to No. 10 following his loss at the Championships, his lowest position since 2008.

Murray stated he was extending his association with Amélie Mauresmo until the conclusion of the US Open before the North American hard court swing, but that he was ideally seeking a long-term agreement. Additionally, he disclosed that he had only recently started training again after having back surgery in September. In consecutive quarterfinal appearances at the Canadian Open and Cincinnati Masters, Murray fell to eventual champions Roger Federer and Jo Wilfried Tsonga despite being up a break in the match's decisive set in each instance. After defeating Jo Wilfried Tsonga in the previous round to record his first top-ten victory of the year, he advanced to the 2014 US Open quarterfinals before falling to Novak Djokovic. Murray didn't make it to a grand slam final for the first time since 2009 during this campaign. Murray thus dropped out of the top 10 positions in the rankings for the first time since June 2008.

Murray entered as the number two seed on a wildcard at the first-ever Shenzhen Open in China. After a hiatus of 14 months following his Wimbledon victory, Murray reached his first final of the year with victories over Somdev Devvarman, Luká Lacko, and Juan Mónaco. He competed against Tommy Robredo of Spain in the championship match, their second meeting. Robredo's decline in fitness eventually proved to be the deciding factor as Murray went on to win the title in three sets after preserving five championship points in the second set tiebreak. He subsequently carried his winning streak to Beijing, where he advanced to the semifinals before falling to Djokovic in straight sets. However, despite being set up, David Ferrer defeated him in the third round of the Shanghai Masters. Murray entered the Vienna Open as a wildcard after leaving Shanghai early to qualify for the ATP World Tour Finals. He advanced to the final, where he met Ferrer once more and won in three sets to win his second championship of the year and 30th overall. Murray advanced to his third final in five weeks after defeating Ferrer once more in the Valencia Open semifinals, strengthening his case for a spot in the season-ending event in London. In a rematch of the Shenzhen Open final, Murray defeated Tommy Robredo in three sets while saving five championship points. After that, Murray advanced to the quarterfinals of the Paris Masters before being defeated by Djokovic in what was the Serbian's 23rd match in only 37 days. He had already been assured a place at the ATP World Tour Finals, though, with to his victory against Dimitrov in the third round.

Murray lost to Kei Nishikori in his initial round-robin encounter at the ATP World Tour Finals but defeated Milos Raonic in his subsequent round. He had his biggest defeat since falling to Djokovic at the 2007 Miami Masters, losing in straight sets against Federer in their last group encounter. As a result, he was eliminated from the event.

Murray mutually decided to separate ways with longtime backroom personnel, training partner Dani Vallverdu, and fitness coach Jez Green when the season ended. They had been with him for five and seven years, respectively, but it was said that they were both dissatisfied with the lack of communication around the hiring of Mauresmo. Murray represented the Manila Mavericks in the first season of the International Premier Tennis League. In February, the team selected Murray as an icon player. The first three games of the event, which were all held in Manila, featured Murray.

2015 Davis Cup Winner And World No. 2 Return

Murray won an exhibition contest in Abu Dhabi to start the year. He later competed alongside Heather Watson in the Hopman Cup, and although winning both of his singles matches in straight sets, they came in second place in their group to Poland.

Murray at the 2015 Australian Open

The Australian Open was his first competitive event of the year. Before upsetting the 11th seed Grigor Dimitrov to get to the quarterfinals, he won his first three matches in straight sets. After victories against Nick Kyrgios and Tomas Berdych, Murray advanced to his fourth event final (three of which came against Djokovic) and ninth grand slam final overall. Although he was defeated by Novak Djokovic in the championship match in four sets, his journey to the final saw him reclaim a spot in the top four of the global rankings for the first time in a year.

Murray then competed in the Rotterdam Open as the top seed, but he lost to Gilles Simon in the quarterfinals, snapping Murray's 12-match losing skid. Murray next competed in the Dubai Championships, where he lost to 18-year-old Borna 'ori' in the quarterfinals once more, dropping him to No. 5 behind Rafael Nadal and Kei Nishikori. Murray then competed in the Davis Cup World Group match against the United States in Glasgow. He defeated both John Isner and Donald Young in his matches, advancing Great Britain to the quarterfinals for the second time in a row with a 3-2 advantage against the Americans.

Murray then advanced to the 2015 Indian Wells semifinals, breaking Tim Henman's record of 496 career victories to become the British man with the most victories in the Open Era.

However, he lost against Djokovic in straight sets for the sixth time in a row. In the 2015 Miami Open semifinals, Murray won his 500th career match, becoming the first British player to achieve 500 or more victories in the Open Era. He ultimately fell to Djokovic in the championship match, this time in three sets. Initially, on a five-week trial, Murray recruited Jonas Björkman to his coaching team in March to fill in for Mauresmo, who had only committed to work with him for 25 weeks.

While Björkman would serve as Murray's primary coach for the entirety of the grass-court season and the US hard-court swing, Mauresmo would only be there for Wimbledon, as she had revealed to him that she was pregnant after the Australian Open.

At the 2015 BMW Open, Murray claimed his first ATP victory on a clay surface. He defeated German Philipp Kohlschreiber in three tight sets to become the first Briton to win a tour-level clay-court match since Buster Mottram in 1976. The following week, he defeated Raonic and Nishikori to go to his second clay-court final at the Madrid Open, marking just his second and third victory on the surface over players ranked in the top 10. He won the clay court Masters 1000 championship and the Madrid title in the final, defeating Rafael Nadal in straight sets. The victory marked Murray's first against Nadal on a clay surface and his first over Federer, Djokovic, or Nadal since Wimbledon in 2013.

At the Italian Open, Murray extended his winning run by defeating Jeremy Chardy in straight sets in his opening encounter. However, Murray later withdrew due to exhaustion after playing nine matches in the previous ten days. After reaching his third French Open semi-final, Murray fell to Djokovic in five sets after making a comeback attempt from two sets to love down, snapping his

15-match winning streak on clay. Murray won a record-tying fourth Queen's Club championship to open his grass court season after overcoming the powerfully serving South African Kevin Anderson in straight sets. Murray lost just two sets in the 2015 Wimbledon Championships, the third grand slam of the year, en route to securing a matchup with Roger Federer in the semifinals. Murray only earned one break point during the whole encounter before falling to the Swiss veteran in straight sets.

Murray returned to Queen's Club following Wimbledon to compete for Great Britain versus France in the Davis Cup quarterfinal match. James Ward's straight-sets loss against Gilles Simon put Great Britain down 1-0 in the match, but Murray even things up by defeating Jo-Wilfried Tsonga. The doubles match was won by Murray and his brother Jamie, who overcame a set deficit to upset Tsonga and Nicolas Mahut in four sets and give

Britain a decisive 2-1 lead heading into the final day. Then, in the fourth rubber, he met Simon. After falling by a set and a break at first, he unexpectedly regained his form again at the end of the second set and went on to win in four sets, taking 12 of the final 15 games (with Simon struggling from an ankle injury). This led Great Britain to their first Davis Cup semi-final since 1981 with a 3-1 advantage against France.

As the top seed and event favorite, Murray next competed at the Citi Open (for the first time since 2006). Despite having served for the match, he lost his opening match to No. 53 Teymuraz Gabashvili in a final set tiebreak. He played doubles with Daniel Nestor, but they were defeated in the opening round by Rohan Bopanna and Florin Mergea, the fourth seeds, also in three sets.

Following this setback, he won the Montreal Masters Rogers Cup by defeating Nishikori in the semifinals and Tsonga in the quarterfinals. Then, he won in three sets in the championship match against Djokovic. His two-year, eight-match losing run to Djokovic ended with this (his last win against him being in the final of Wimbledon in 2013). He overtook Federer in terms of rankings after winning the match, moving up to No. 2 for the first time in more than two years. In doubles, he teamed up with Leander Paes, and they defeated Chardy and Anderson in their opening match before falling to Jamie and John Peers in two sets. This was the first time the Murray brothers had faced off against each other in a Tour-level match, and Andy described the encounter as "awkward" and Jamie described it as "a bit weird."

In the Cincinnati Masters, the second Master Series event of the US Hard Court season, Murray defeated veteran Mardy Fish in the second round before defeating Grigor Dimitrov and Richard

Gasquet in three-set matches. On both occasions, Murray had to rally from a set down, with Dimitrov serving for the match in the deciding set. Murray lost in straight sets against the reigning champion Roger Federer in the semi-final, and as a result of Federer's eventual victory, Murray's ranking and seeding for the US Open dropped to No. 3. Murray tied Roger Federer's record of eight victories from two sets to love down at the US Open when he defeated Nick Kyrgios in four sets before defeating Adrian Mannarino in five sets after trailing two sets to none. After defeating Thomaz Bellucci in straight sets, he lost to Kevin Anderson in the fourth round in four sets. Since losing to Stan Wawrinka in the third round of the 2010 US Open, Murray has reached 18 straight Grand Slam quarterfinals (excluding his absence from the 2013 French Open). This streak lasted for five years.

Murray defeated Thanasi Kokkinakis and Bernard Tomic in both of his singles rubbers during his match against Australia in the Davis Cup World Group semifinals in Glasgow.

He also played with his brother Jamie, and the two of them defeated Sam Groth and Lleyton Hewitt in five sets. The victory helped Great Britain advance to the Davis Cup final for the first time since 1978 with a 3-2 advantage over Australia. Murray reached the finals of the Paris Masters with just one set lost after defeating Borna ori, David Goffin, and David Ferrer. Murray had previously lost in straight sets against Djokovic in the semifinals of the Shanghai Masters. He joined Novak Djokovic, Roger Federer, and Rafael Nadal as the only players to advance to the semifinals (or better) in all nine ATP World Tour Masters 1000 events after defeating Richard Gasquet in three sets. He also made sure that he recorded his best match record in a single season. Then, he was defeated by Djokovic in the championship match in three sets.

Murray, the No. 2 player in the world, competed in the ATP World Tour Finals in London and was paired with Stan Wawrinka, David Ferrer, and Rafael Nadal in the Ilie Năstase group. After beating Ferrer and losing to Nadal and Wawrinka in the round-robin stage, he was eliminated. Federer, though, concluded the season ranked No. 2 for the first time after failing to win the competition.

In the Davis Cup final, Kyle Edmund had lost the opening singles rubber in five sets when Murray defeated Ruben Bemelmans in straight sets. The match was played on indoor clay courts in Ghent. After defeating David Goffin once more in the reverse singles on Sunday, he helped his brother Jamie and Great Britain win the Davis Cup 3-1, their first since 1936 and eleventh overall. They defeated the team of Steve Darcis and David Goffin in four sets. Murray also joined John McEnroe and Mats Wilander as the only players to have won all eight of their singles rubbers in a Davis Cup season since the current Davis Cup system was implemented.

2016: Second Wimbledon and Olympic Gold, and ascent to world No. 1

Murray competed in the Hopman Cup to start the 2016 campaign, teaming up once more with Heather Watson. Nevertheless, they came in second place in their group after losing to eventual winners Nick Kyrgios and Daria Gavrilova of Australia in their encounter.

Murray participated at the Australian Open, where he was trying to capture his first championship there after four runner-up finishes, in his first competitive match of 2016. With victories against

Alexander Zverev, Sam Groth, Joo Sousa, Bernard Tomic, David Ferrer, and Milos Raonic—while lost four sets along the way—he went on to reach his seventh Australian Open final. He was unable to earn his maiden championship, however, as he was defeated in the final by an in-form Novak Djokovic (who won a record-tying sixth title) in straight sets. The match was a replay of the previous year's final. He was the first person to lose five Grand Slam finals in a single tournament during the Open Era (the other being Ivan Lendl). Murray then hired Jamie Delgado as an assistant coach in February.

Murray then competed in the 2016 Davis Cup, defeating Kei Nishikori in five sets and Taro Daniel in straight sets. Murray then participated in the 2016 Indian Wells Masters, the first Masters 1000 of the year. In the second round, he overcame Marcel Granollers in straight sets, but in the third round, he lost to Federico Delbonis right away.

Murray then competed as the second seed at the 2016 Miami Open. In the second round, he overcame Denis Istomin in straight sets. However, after winning the opening set against 26th seed Grigor Dimitrov, he lost the match in the first set.

At the 2016 Monte-Carlo Rolex Masters, Murray started his clay court season as the second seed. Murray fought against Pierre-Hugues Herbert in the second round, but Murray prevailed in three sets. With a set and two breaks behind against the 16th seed Benoît Paire in the third round, Murray battled once again. Paire also had a game-tying serve in the third set, but Murray prevailed in three sets. In the quarterfinals, Murray won in straight sets over Milos Raonic, the 10th seed. Murray won the opening set against Rafael Nadal, the fifth seed and eventual winner, but lost in the semifinals. The next year, Murray participated in the Mutua Madrid Open as the second seed and reigning champion.

Radek Tpánek, a qualifier, was beaten by Murray in three sets. After eliminating the 16th seed Gilles Simon and the eighth seed Tomas Berdych in straight sets, he moved on to the semifinals. Murray, who had already lost to Nadal earlier in the year, overcame him in straight sets in the semifinals. Novak Djokovic, the top seed, defeated Murray in the championship match in three sets. Due to this defeat, Murray's ATP ranking slipped from second to third. A short while afterward, Mauresmo and Murray jointly said that they had "mutually agreed" to stop their coaching collaboration.

In the 2016 Wimbledon final, Murray defeated Milos Raonic 6-4, 7-6(3), and 7-6(2) to win his second Wimbledon championship.

After winning the 2016 Internazionali BNL d'Italia for his first championship of the year and 36th overall, Murray was once again ranked second.

Mikhail Kukushkin, Jérémy Chardy, Lucas Pouille, David Goffin, the 12th seed, and Novak Djokovic were all upset by him in straight sets. Being the first British player to win the championship since Virginia Wade in 1971 and the first British man to do it since George Patrick Hughes in 1931, this was his first victory against Djokovic on clay. Murray then proceeded to the French Open, where he battled in the initial rounds until defeating Czech wildcard Jiri Tpánek and Frenchman Mathias Bourgue in two five-set victories. He defeated John Isner and Ivo Karlovic, two strong servers, in straight sets to get to the quarterfinals, where he defeated local favorite Richard Gasquet in four games to earn a matchup with reigning champion Stanislas Wawrinka. For the first time since Bunny Austin in 1937, Murray overcame Wawrinka in four sets to go to the French Open final. He was beaten by Djokovic in the French Open final for the first time, dropping the match in four sets.

Ivan Lendl consented to take up Murray's old position as coach in June 2016. At the 2016 Aegon Championships, Murray began his season on grass as the top seed and defending champion. Despite having a set point in the first set and three set points in the second, Murray overcame Nicolas Mahut in straight sets. He then overcame Alja Bedene, a fellow countryman, in straight sets. The No. 5 seed Marin Ili and another countryman, Kyle Edmund, were defeated by him three sets later. He trailed third-seeded Milos Raonic by a set and a break in the championship match. Murray nevertheless managed to return and capture a record-tying fifth Queen's Club Championship, his second in 2016. Murray then competed as the second seed in the 2016 Wimbledon Championships, the third major of the year. In the first four rounds, Murray defeated Liam Broady, Lu Yen-Hsun, John Millman, and Nick Kyrgios in straight sets. To get to his third consecutive major final, Murray then overcame the 10th seed Tomá Berdych in straight sets after defeating the 12th seed Jo-Wilfried Tsonga in five sets in the quarterfinal. On July 10, Murray defeated Raonic in the championship match to earn his second Wimbledon championship and third major championship overall. His victory at Wimbledon marked his third victory of the year and 38th Tour victory overall.

Murray Then Participated In The Olympic Games In Rio.

He defeated Juan Martin del Potro in the over-four-hour final to become the first athlete, male or female, to win two consecutive gold medals in tennis singles competitions. His victory marked his fourth championship of the year and third in a row. Murray won his first four matches at the US Open by defeating Grigor Dimitrov, Lukas Rosol, Marcel Granollers, and Paolo Lorenzi. Despite having two sets to one lead, his streak came to an end as he was defeated in five sets by sixth seed Kei Nishikori.

His subsequent endeavor was the 2016 Davis Cup semifinal matchup versus Argentina in Glasgow. In five sets, he was defeated by Juan Martin del Potro in the opening match. He joined up with his brother Jamie to defeat del Potro and Leonardo Mayer in the third rubber in four sets after Great Britain also lost the second match. He subsequently defeated Guido Pella in the fourth rubber in a straight-sets victory, although Great Britain ultimately lost the match. The next year, Murray won the China Open for his 40th career tour victory and fifth victory in 2016. Andrey Kuznetsov, Kyle Edmund, David Ferrer, and Grigor Dimitrov were all beaten by him in straight sets. To win the Shanghai Rolex Masters and earn his third championship in Shanghai, Murray first defeated Steve Johnson, Lucas Pouille, David Goffin, Gilles Simon, and Roberto Bautista

Agut in straight sets. With 41 Tour titles each, this was his sixth victory of the year, tying him for 15th place on the Open Era championships tally with former No. 1 Stefan Edberg.

Murray won the Erste Bank Open for his eighth tour championship of the 2016 season, extending his winning run to 15 games. In the first two rounds of his event, he defeated Martin Klizan and Gilles Simon in three sets. However, Murray advanced to the final thanks to a convincing victory over John Isner in the quarterfinal and a walkover after David Ferrer withdrew due to a leg injury. He defeated Jo-Wilfried Tsonga there, winning his third straight championship. Murray broke a tie with former No. 1 Stefan Edberg and became the first player in the Open Era to win seven trophies in a single season. He also moved to sole 15th place on the list of all-time singles victories.

If Djokovic did not advance to the final, Murray knew going into the Paris Masters that a victory would be enough to elevate him to the position of world No. 1 for the first time. After defeating Fernando Verdasco and Lucas Pouille to go to the quarterfinals, Murray met Berdych and won in straight sets to advance to the semifinals. Murray would overtake Djokovic as the number one player if he made it to the final because Djokovic fell to Marin Cilic. He had Milos Raonic on his mind for the semifinal match. But before the game began, Raonic pulled out, giving Murray a walkover. Murray as a consequence became the first British guy to hold the top spot since the rankings' inception in 1973. Murray then won the Paris Masters and his fourth straight event by defeating John Isner in the championship match in three sets. In November 2016, Murray made his first appearance in the ATP World Tour Finals final before defeating Novak Djokovic in two sets. This victory propelled Murray to the tournament's year-end No. 1 ranking and made him the first person to win a Grand Slam, the ATP World Tour Finals, the men's singles competition at the Olympics, and a Masters 1000 championship in the same calendar year. For the first time, Murray received recognition from the International Tennis Federation as their 2016 ITF Men's World Champion.

2017: Struggles with form and injury, and hiatus

For his contributions to tennis and philanthropy, Murray received a knighthood in the 2017 New Year's Honours, making him the UK's youngest knight aged 29. After losing to David Goffin in the Mubadala World Tennis Championship semifinals to begin the season, he went on to defeat Milos Raonic in the third-place play-off. Murray then advanced to the Qatar Open final, where he was defeated by Novak Djokovic in three sets despite having preserved three title points. He was defeated by Mischa Zverev in the fourth round of the Australian Open in four sets. In February, Murray made a comeback in the Dubai Duty-Free Tennis Championships competition. There, he defeated Fernando Verdasco in straight sets to win his lone title of the year, although nearly fell to Philipp Kohlschreiber in the quarterfinals, when Murray had to save seven match chances. The next week, he was shockingly defeated by Vasek Pospisil in the second round of the Indian Wells Masters.

Murray returned to play at the Monte Carlo Masters in April after missing a month due to an elbow injury, however, he was defeated by Albert Ramos-Vinolas in the third round. Then he competed in Barcelona, where Dominic Thiem defeated him in the semifinal match. Murray lost to Borna Coric in the third round of the Madrid event and to Fabio Fognini in the second round of the Rome tournament, where he was the reigning champion, as he continued to struggle. He lost both of these matches without taking a set. At the 2017 French Open, Murray overcame Juan Martin del Potro and Karen Khachanov in straight sets after battling through a four-set victory over Andrey Kuznetsov and Martin Kilian in the preliminary stages. He overcame Kei Nishikori in the quarterfinals in four sets, but Stan Wawrinka prevailed in the semifinals in five sets.

Murray, a five-time winner at Queens, committed his prize money to the Grenfell Tower disaster victims, but Jordan Thompson beat him in straight sets in the opening round.

He returned to Wimbledon as the reigning champion despite worries about a persistent hip ailment, and he advanced to the third round with victories against Dustin Brown and Alexander Bublik in straight sets. Fabio Fognini won the opening set of the tournament for him, but he won the next four sets to advance. [369] Murray defeated Benoit Paire in straight sets to go to the quarterfinals. Sam Querrey, though, upset him in five sets in the quarterfinal.

Due to his hip injury, Murray missed the Canadian Open and the Cincinnati Masters, which caused him to lose his top spot to Rafael Nadal. The 2017 US Open was the first Grand Slam tournament he had missed since the 2013 French Open as a result of his injury, which caused him to withdraw from the competition two days before the tournament's start. Murray then withdrew from the Asian hardcourt swing and declared that it was "most likely" that he would not participate in a professional tournament again in 2017. In the end, he did not play again after pulling out of Paris, which prevented him from earning a spot in the 2017 ATP Finals. That November, as a result of his inactivity, his ranking dropped significantly to No. 16, its lowest position since May 2008. In Glasgow, Murray returned to the court to face Federer in a charity match, and he announced his desire to rejoin the tour in Brisbane. He and Ivan Lendl stated that they had again mutually terminated their coaching relationship the following week.

2018: Hip Surgery, 800th Place Finish, And Tour Comeback

Due to a hip issue, Murray withdrew from the Australian Open and Brisbane International.

Murray described the treatment as one possibility for healing in a post on Instagram. He continued by saying that hip surgery was an alternative but that the likelihood of success was lower. Murray revealed on Instagram on January 8 that he had undergone hip surgery.

Kyle Edmund defeated Murray to become the first British No. 1 since 2006 in March. Later that month, Murray posted images of himself practicing against British junior player Aidan McHugh on Instagram and said he was improving after many days of competing at the Mouratoglou Academy in Nice. At the Rosmalen Grass Court Championships in June, he then said that he would play his first ATP tournament following hip surgery. However, he later withdrew, claiming he was not yet ready and wanted to be 100%. He did, however, afterward declare that he will compete again in the Queen's Club Championships. Then, in the opening round, he was defeated in three sets by Nick Kyrgios. The Eastbourne International gave him a wildcard, and he used it to defeat Stan Wawrinka in the first round before falling to Kyle Edmund in the second. A day before the competition, he announced his withdrawal from Wimbledon, stating it was too soon to play five-set matches. This withdrawal caused him to slide to 839th in the ATP rankings, which was his most recent low position since he initially joined the rankings on July 21, 2003.

He subsequently competed at the Washington Open, where he defeated Mackenzie McDonald in the opening round in three sets. The next opponent was Kyle Edmund, who had previously defeated him at Eastbourne, and beat him in three sets. After winning in three sets over Marius Copil in the third round of play in a match that lasted until well after 3 AM local time, Murray broke down in tears. To complete his rehabilitation and concentrate on the Cincinnati Masters, for which he had a wildcard, he withdrew from the competition as well as the Canadian Open the following week. He ultimately fell to France's Lucas Pouille in the opening round, losing in three sets.

At the US Open, Murray won his first grand slam match since 2013, defeating Australian James Duckworth in four sets.

He was unable to advance, falling to Fernando Verdasco of Spain in the second round in four sets.

To continue his recovery from his injury, Murray withdrew from Great Britain's Davis Cup match against Uzbekistan in Glasgow.

He used a wildcard to enter the Shenzhen Open. Zhizhen Zhang retired in the third set of the first round, which allowed him to proceed to the second round. There, he took on top seed and reigning champion David Goffin, who Murray defeated in straight sets. After that, he lost in straight sets to Fernando Verdasco in the quarterfinals. Murray had been scheduled to compete at the China Open the following week, but after experiencing a minor ankle injury, he opted to call it quits on the current campaign to ensure his fitness for the next year.

2019: Second hip surgery, come back, and the first title in two years

To be better prepared for Brisbane International, Murray arrived in Brisbane early. He defeated James Duckworth in the first round in straight sets, although he afterward acknowledged that he was unsure of how long he would be able to play tennis of the highest caliber. The 16th-ranked player in the world at the time, Daniil Medvedev, beat Murray in the following round.

At a news conference on January 11, 2019, shortly before the Australian Open, an emotional Murray said he may retire from tennis because he has struggled physically for a "long time,", especially with his hip problem. He claimed that he had been dealing with hip pain every day, which made it difficult for him to do things like put on his shoes and socks. He mentioned the prospect of undergoing a second hip operation but voiced skepticism that this would be an effective strategy to extend his career rather than just "have a better quality of life, and be free of pain." He said he wanted to make it to Wimbledon, but if he could not make it until the summer, "I'm not sure I can play through the agony for another four or five months," the Australian Open may be his last match.

Murray's declaration was met with praise from both active and former tennis players, including Juan Martin del Potro, Kyle Edmund, Billie Jean King, and the other members of the "Big Four."

Murray competed in the Australian Open singles, but he lost his opening match to Roberto Bautista

Agut, the 22nd seed, in a four-hour, five-set "epic." In honor of his upcoming retirement, a video montage of tributes starring other elite athletes, including Roger Federer, Novak Djokovic, Sloane Stephens, and Caroline Wozniacki, aired after the match. He admitted to pondering a second hip operation in the post-game interview and said he hadn't decided if he would play again after the procedure.

Bob Bryan persuaded Murray to undergo the "Birmingham hip (BHR)" procedure, which involved placing a cobalt-chrome metal cap over the femur and a matching metal cup in the acetabulum, in August 2018. (a conservative bone-saving alternative to a traditional Total Hip Replacement). Murray was told by Bryan that the BHR would enhance his quality of life and perhaps enable him to make a comeback to the professional tennis circuit. Murray said on Instagram on January

29 that he had undergone hip resurfacing surgery in London, hoping that it would "put an end to my hip discomfort." Professor Derek McMinn, who developed the BHR implant and operation, stated on February 4 in an interview with The Times that Murray's prospects of returning to competitive tennis should be "in the upper 90%."

In an interview on March 7, Murray said he had undergone surgery to remove his hip pain and was now pain-free. He added that he might now resume playing competitive tennis, but any potential return to Wimbledon would depend on how his hip felt. Murray also said he would not rush his comeback and might test his condition by playing doubles.

Two years after being given the honor, Murray received his knighthood from Prince Charles at Buckingham Palace on May 16, 2019.

In June, Murray made a comeback to the tennis world professionals by competing in the Queen's Club Championships doubles match with Feliciano Lopez.

The team defeated top seeds Juan Sebastián Cabal and Robert Farah in straight sets in the first round. In the semifinals, they defeated John Peers and Henri Kontinen, the reigning champions. Rajeev Ram and Joe Salisbury were defeated by Murray and Lopez in a final set champions tiebreak to claim the title. Murray said his "hip felt terrific" and "there was no soreness" after the victory. At Eastbourne International, Murray began his recovery from injury by competing in the doubles event with Marcelo Melo, where they were defeated by Cabal and Farah in the opening round. In the men's doubles and mixed doubles competitions at the 2019 Wimbledon Championships, Murray participated. He played with Pierre-Hugues Herbert in the men's doubles and lost to them in the second round. In the mixed doubles, he lost to top seeds Bruno Soares and Nicole Melichar in the third round.

In the Citi Open doubles tournament that followed Murray's Wimbledon run, Andy and his brother Jamie overcame Edouard Roger-Vasselin and Nicolas Mahut before falling to Michael Venus and Raven Klaasen in the round of 16.

His combination with Feliciano Lopez was retained for his subsequent match at the Canadian Open, where they overcame Marcelo Melo and Lukasz Kubot but fell short against Fabrice Martin and Jeremy Chardy. After the competition, Murray announced his comeback to singles play at the Western & Southern Open and shared his ambitions to compete in China the next fall.

Murray met Richard Gasquet in the opening round of the 2019 Cincinnati Masters, his first singles match since the 2019 Australian Open, and lost in straight sets. In just the second match of their senior careers, Andy Murray and Feliciano López faced Jamie Murray and Neal Skupski in the quarterfinal of the Cincinnati doubles tournament. Jamie and Skupski won in three sets to advance, and Andy Murray said in the wake of the match that he would now focus his efforts on making a comeback to the singles tour. After that, Murray participated in the 2019 Winston-Salem Open, where his opening-round opponent was Tennys Sandgren. Although the score was tight, Murray lost in straight sets. Murray then considered going to the Challenger division, missing the US Open completely, and concentrating on two events that were taking place at the same time. Murray chose to compete in the Rafa Nadal Open Banc Sabadell Challenger event in 2019, marking his first appearance on the lower-level Challenger Tour since 2005. Murray won his first singles match since hip surgery by defeating 17-year-old Imran Sibille in the opening round of the competition in just under 43 minutes and straight sets. In the third round, Matteo Viola defeated him.

In the second round of the inaugural Zhuhai Championships in September 2019, Murray was defeated by eventual champion Alex de Minaur. He also competed in the China Open, where he defeated world No. 13 Matteo Berrettini, but was defeated in the quarterfinals by eventual winner Dominic Thiem. After losing to 12th-ranked Fabio Fognini in the second round of the Shanghai Open, Murray went on to win his first championship since surgery at the European Open in October 2019 by defeating three-time Grand Slam champion Stan Wawrinka. He was selected for the squad for the 2019 Davis Cup finals in November 2019, which allowed him to play for Great Britain for the first time since 2016. He was only able to play one rubber during Great Britain's journey to the semifinals, though.

The television documentary Andy Murray: Resurfacing, which covered Murray's attempts to recover from his hip injury over two years from his Wimbledon loss in 2017 to his doubles triumph at Queen's Club in 2019, was published on the Amazon Prime platform at the end of November 2019.

Murray's camp said in late December that the pelvic ailment that had limited his participation in the Davis Cup will also keep him out of the forthcoming 2020 Australian Open and the first-ever ATP Cup.

2020: First top 10 wins in three years

Numerous tournaments on the 2020 ATP Tour were either postponed or canceled as a result of the COVID-19 epidemic. Murray competed in his first ATP event of 2020 in the Western & Southern Open in August, where he had a wildcard entry. After defeating world No. 7 Alexander Zverev in the second round, he defeated Frances Tiafoe in the opening round. This was his first triumph against a top-10 player in more than three years and the 102nd of his career. He was defeated by Milos Raonic in straight sets in the third round.

In his first-round encounter at the US Open without spectators, Yoshihito Nishioka of Japan was barely defeated by Murray after falling behind by two sets.

Then, in the second round, he was defeated by Canadian Felix Auger-Aliassime, the 15th seed, in straight sets.

He subsequently joined the French Open as a wildcard but lost to Stan Wawrinka in the opening round in straight sets.

Murray competed in his last match of the year at the Bett1Hulks Indoors, where he was given a wildcard into the main draw and fell to Fernando Verdasco in the opening round in straight sets. He did not participate in the European Open, failing to successfully defend his title.

2021: Wimbledon third round

Murray was scheduled to begin his season at the 2021 Australian Open as a wildcard, however, after testing positive for COVID-19 on January 14, this was called into question. His absence from the Australian Open was officially announced on January 22 due to his inability to locate a suitable quarantine following his positive test.

The 2021 Open Sud de France was his first competition of the year, and as a wildcard, he was eliminated in the first round. After that, in March, he participated as a wildcard in the 2021 ABN AMRO World Tennis Tournament in Rotterdam, where he was defeated by Andrey Rublev in the second round.

Due to a groin injury, Murray was mainly idle for the following three months. He only managed to play in two doubles matches at the Italian Open in May. His rating was too low as a result of a straight admission into the French Open. He chose to concentrate on the next grass court season rather than join qualifying or attempt to obtain a wild card.

He made a comeback to singles competition at the Queen's Club Championships as a wildcard, where he beat Benoît Paire in the opening round before falling to the top seed, Matteo Berrettini, in the second round in straight sets.

He was given a wildcard to Wimbledon. He defeated qualifier Oscar Otte and the 24th seed Nikoloz Basilashvili before falling to Denis Shapovalov in the third round.

Murray was the two-time defending champion in the men's singles and men's doubles events at the 2020 Summer Olympics. Murray was paired with Canadian Félix Auger-Aliassime, the world's No. 15, however, Auger-Aliassime withdrew before their first-round singles match due to a quadriceps strain, choosing instead to participate in the doubles match instead. Max Purcell, an Australian, took Murray's position and eventually defeated Auger-Aliassime. After defeating the French pair Nicolas Mahut and Pierre-Hugues Herbert in the first round and the German pair Kevin Krawietz and Tim Pütz in the second, Murray and partner Joe Salisbury advanced to the men's doubles quarterfinals before losing to the Croatian pair and eventual silver medalists Marin ili and Ivan Dodig.

Murray participated in two US circuit events.

At the Western & Southern Open in 2021, Murray defeated Richard Gasquet in straight sets as a wildcard before falling to Hubert Hurkacz in the second round.

In the first round of the 2021 Winston-Salem Open, Murray used a wildcard entry once more to defeat Noah Rubin (who replaced Nick Kyrgios, who withdrew just before the match began), before falling to Frances Tiafoe in the second. In the first round of the US Open, he was defeated by Stefanos Tsitsipas in five sets. The match was contentious because Tsitsipas had an eight-minute toilet break during it, and Murray accused Tsitsipas of cheating.

Murray then accepted a wildcard to play in the 2021 Open de Rennes, an ATP Challenger Tour competition.

In the first round, he overcame Yannick Maden in straight sets, but he fell to Roman Safiullin in three sets.

Murray then competed in the Moselle Open as a wildcard, making it to the quarterfinals before falling to Hubert Hurkacz of Poland, the eventual winner, and top seed. At the 2021 San Diego Open, Murray also suffered a loss as a wildcard in the round of 16 to second-seeded Casper Ruud, who went on to win the tournament. Another wildcard was given to him for the Indian Wells Masters, where he advanced to the third round before losing to Alexander Zverev. After defeating Frances Tiafoe in a marathon match that lasted three hours and forty-five minutes, he advanced as a wildcard to the second round of the European Open. In the second round, he was defeated in straight sets by Diego Schwartzman. Murray, a wildcard participant at the Vienna Open, defeated Hubert Hurkacz, the fifth seed and world No. 10, in the first round in three sets to earn his 103rd career top-10 victory and the first of the year. However, he lost in straight sets against Carlos Alcaraz in the next round. He defeated top seed and World No. 10 Jannik Sinner at the 2021 Stockholm Open to advance to the quarterfinals as a wildcard, earning him his second top-ten victory in two weeks, his second of the season, and the 104th of his career.

2022: First ATP finals since 2019, 700th match win, and return to top 50

"Many people said I wouldn't be able to play again, and many others said I would be able to hit tennis balls but wouldn't be able to compete again. That was absurd, and I want to see how near the top of the game I can return to."

Murray talks openly about his problems and his healing.

In December, Murray competed in the 2021 Mubadala World Tennis Championship, an exhibition match. After prevailing in straight sets over Dan Evans, he played Rafael Nadal in their first encounter since the 2016 Madrid Open semifinals. He won in straight sets against Nadal. Andrey Rublev defeated Murray in the championship match in straight sets and a tiebreak.

Murray reached the final at the Sydney Tennis Classic as a wildcard after falling to Facundo Bagnis in the first round of the Melbourne Summer Set. He did so by defeating Viktor Durasovic in the first round and second-seeded Nikoloz Basilashvili in the second round in a match that lasted more than three hours. He defeated Reilly Opelka in the semifinals before losing to Aslan Karatsev in the championship match when his quarterfinal opponent, the eighth seed David Goffin, quit due to injury.

As a wildcard, Murray took part in the 2022 Australian Open. Murray won the opening round in five sets as he faced Nikoloz Basilashvili for the second time in a week. In the second round, he was defeated by Taro Daniel in straight sets and lost.

Murray won a wildcard to compete in the 2022 Rotterdam Open when he decided to conclude his trial term with new coach Jan de Witt. In the first round, he defeated Alexander Bublik, but in the second, he was defeated by Félix Auger-Aliassime. Dani Vallverdu was also employed by him as a substitute coach. Murray was a wildcard entry for the 2022 Qatar Open. He faced Taro Daniel in a repeat of the Australian Open's second round, which Murray won in straight sets. For the first time since he was defeated by Novak Djokovic in the Miami Open final in 2015, Murray received a bagel after losing his second-round match to second-seeded Roberto Bautista Agut 6-0, 6-1.

Following Qatar, Murray competed in the 2022 Dubai Tennis Championships as a wildcard to win the tournament for the first time in five years. He defeated Jannik Sinner in straight sets but lost to Christopher O'Connell. Murray rehired Ivan Lendl, who he had previously worked with twice, as his coach after his time at Vallverdu came to an end.

Taro Daniel and Murray met for the third time in 2022 in the first round of the 2022 Indian Wells Masters, which Murray joined as a wildcard in March. He defeated Daniel in three sets, earning his 700th victory overall, but fell to Alexander Bublik in the next round in straight sets. Murray defeated Federico Delbonis in straight sets to earn a wildcard to the Miami Open in 2022. In the second round, he was defeated by top seed and world No. 2 Daniil Medvedev in straight sets.

Murray initially said in February that he intended to forgo the Spring clay season, but he subsequently changed his mind and agreed to accept a wildcard for the 2022 Madrid Open in April. Murray defeated Dominic Thiem and Denis Shapovalov in the opening two rounds of the 2022 Madrid Open to set up a matchup with Novak Djokovic for the first time in five years. Djokovic received a walkover as Murray subsequently withdrew from the match owing to a stomach ailment.

In his first competition after his return, Murray competed in the challenger event in Surbiton, where he advanced to the quarterfinals before falling to Denis Kudla in three sets. After defeating Chris O'Connell and the 7th seed Alexander Bublik in Stuttgart, Murray defeated first seed and world No. 5 Stefanos Tsitsipas in straight sets to win his first match against a top 5 player since 2016. After defeating Nick Kyrgios in straight sets, he advanced to the championship match but fell to Matteo Berrettini in three sets. Murray's rating climbed to No. 47 as a consequence, making his first appearance in the top 50 since 2018. However, he had to leave the Queen's Club Championships due to an injury he got in the final.

At Wimbledon, Murray defeated 20th seed John Isner in the second round after defeating James Duckworth in four sets in the first round. After Wimbledon, he competed in the Hall of Fame Open, where he advanced to the quarterfinals before falling to third-seeded Alexander Bublik in straight sets.

Murray lost to Mikael Ymer in the Citi Open first round, and then he lost to Taylor Fritz as a wildcard in the Canadian Open first round to start his American hard court swing. Murray participated in a Cincinnati Masters qualifying event for the first time since 2005.

However, Murray was transferred to the main draw where he defeated Stan Wawrinka in three sets to go to the second round as a result of a Special Exempt place being removed from the competition. Murray was defeated by Cameron Norrie in the second round and lost in three sets.

Playing Style

Murray is a defensive baseline player who uses an all-court style of play. According to tennis coach Paul Annacone, Murray "may be the finest counterpuncher on tour right now." He excels in hitting winners from defensive positions thanks to his low mistake rate groundstrokes, quick transition from defense to offense, and ability to anticipate and react. While using his forehand, which is more active, and a sliced backhand to allow opponents to play into his defensive game before playing more aggressively, Murray also boasts one of the greatest two-handed backhands on the tour. Murray may have the finest lob in the game, surpassing Lleyton Hewitt, according to Tim Henman in 2013. Murray frequently uses passive exchanges from the baseline in his strategies. He may surprise opponents who are accustomed to the sluggish rallies by adding surprising speed to his groundstrokes. Murray is one of the best returners in the game and frequently uses his tremendous reach and anticipation to swat back quick serves. Murray is therefore seldom aced.

Murray is renowned for being one of the court's smartest strategists and frequently creating points. His drop shot and net game are two more areas where he excels, but not significantly. He often plays from the baseline, but when he has to complete points more quickly, he will walk up to the net and volley. Although hard courts are his favorite surface, Murray performs best on a fast surface like grass, where he has won eight singles titles, including the Wimbledon Championships and the 2012 Olympic Gold Medal. He has put a lot of effort into developing his clay court technique since 2008, and as a result, he won his first clay court championships in 2015 in Munich and Madrid and advanced to his first French Open final in 2016. While Murray's serve is a key weapon for him—his first serve can occasionally reach speeds of 130 mph or higher and net him several free points—it may become erratic when delivered under duress, particularly with a more flimsy and slowly delivered second serve.

Since the 2011 campaign, Murray has worked to enhance his second serve, forehand, consistency, and mental game, all of which have been essential to his continued success. Murray also played a more attacking style of tennis.

Endorsements And Equipment

Murray and German company Adidas agreed to a five-year, £30 million contract in 2009. Wearing their selection of tennis shoes was part of this. Shiatzy Chen, Royal Bank of Scotland, and Highland Spring were Murray's shirt sleeve sponsors thanks to the partnership with Adidas. He wore Fred Perry clothing up until late 2009 when Adidas signed him. In December 2014, Murray signed a four-year contract with sportswear firm Under Armour, allegedly for $25 million, after Adidas opted not to renew their agreement with him. Before announcing his retirement, Murray inked a contract with Castore for the 2019 season.

Murray utilizes Head rackets and frequently makes appearances in the company's ads. While he promotes the Head Radical Pro model, his real playing racket reportedly has a 16–19 string design and is a pro stock PT57A that has been modified. It is based on the original Pro Tour 630 model. The racquet used to be set up extremely heavy at the beginning of his career, but after a 2007 wrist injury, its weight was lowered.

In June 2012, the Swiss watch manufacturer Rado announced that Murray had signed a deal to wear their D-Star 200 model.

Coaches

Leon Smith (1998–2004), Pato Alvarez (2003–2005), Mark Petchey (2005–2006), Brad Gilbert (2006–2007), Miles Maclagan (2007–2010), lex Corretja (2010–2011), Ivan Lendl (2011–2014, 2016–2017, 2022–), Amélie Mauresmo (2014–2016), Jonas Björkman (2015), and Jamie Delgado have all served as coaches for Murray over the years (2016–2021). He was briefly tutored by Dani Vallverdu in 2022, and he has been coached by Ivan Lendl since March of that year.

Charitable Work

Murray helped David Beckham create the organization in 2009 and is a founding member of the Malaria No More UK Leadership Council. YouTube and the charity's website both include video from the unveiling at Wembley Stadium. Murray also created the brief PSA "Nets Needed" for the charity to assist spread awareness and earning money to support the battle against malaria. Murray has also participated in several tennis-related charitable initiatives, such as the Rally for Relief activities that were held before the 2011 Australian Open.

In a charity doubles match in June 2013 at the Queen's Club in London against Murray's coach and eight-time grand slam winner Ivan Lendl and No. 6 Tomá Berdych, Murray joined up with former British No. 1 Tim Henman. After Ross Hutchins, a fellow British player, and his best friend, received a Hodgkin's lymphoma diagnosis, the Rally Against Cancer event was planned to raise money for the Royal Marsden Cancer Charity. On Sunday, June 16, the event took place after the last day of competitive play at the AEGON Championships. Murray then gave all of his prize money to The Royal Marsden Cancer Charity after winning the competition.

Murray participated in the "Rally for Bally" event in June 2014, which was held in memory of Elena Baltacha, who passed away from liver cancer. At Queen's Club, Murray competed against Heather Watson, Martina Hingis, Victoria Azarenka, and his brother Jamie. The Elena Baltacha Academy of Tennis and the Royal Marsden Cancer Charity both benefited financially from the event. Baltacha's academy students joined Murray on the court for a game. Murray received the 2014 Arthur Ashe

Humanitarian of the Year award for his numerous charity endeavors.

National identity

Oor Wullie's Big Bucket Trail has a sculpture of Oor Wullie portrayed as Andy Murray.

Murray claims to be both British and Scottish. The media has frequently discussed his sense of national identity. When asked whether he was British or Scottish during a cameo on the comedy program Outnumbered, Murray said, "Depends whether I win or not." Before Wimbledon 2006, Murray was quoted as saying that he would "support whoever England is playing" in the World Cup. This comment kicked off a significant portion of the debate surrounding Murray's national identification. The words were made in fun and solely in response to Murray being taunted by writer Des Kelly and Henman over Scotland's inability to qualify, according to English ex-tennis player Tim Henman.

Murray originally refrained from endorsing either side of the Scottish independence question in 2014, recalling the vitriol he had endured following his 2006 remarks about the England-World Cup. Murray posted a statement just before the vote that the media interpreted as being pro-independence. For voicing his views, he was subjected to internet harassment, including communications that Police Scotland described as "vile" and one of which referred to the Dunblane massacre. Murray stated he did not regret expressing his opinion, but that it was out of character and that he would now focus on his tennis career. A few days after the referendum, which saw a 55% majority against Scottish independence, Murray indicated that he would focus on his tennis career in the future.

Victory salute

At Wimbledon 2012, Murray raised both hands in the air and waved them back and forth after defeating Nikolay Davydenko. Murray refused to explain and has since carried on doing this to mark his triumphs. The identical victory salute was used by Murray in 2013 to celebrate his maiden Wimbledon triumph. The true reason, according to Murray, is that I had several friends and family members who were dealing with different problems at the time. I knew they would be watching, and I wanted to let them know I was thinking of them.

Ross Hutchins, a buddy who had been given the news that he had cancer in December 2012, was honored after he won the Brisbane International in January 2013. Hutchins acknowledged that Murray's winning salute was a message for him.

Other

After a match with Kenneth Carlsen in 2006, there was controversy. In the post-match interview, Murray continued to say that he and Carlsen had "played like ladies" during the first set after receiving a warning for racket abuse. Murray received jeers for the remarks but subsequently clarified that it was meant to be a lighthearted retort to what Svetlana Kuznetsova had said at the Hopman Cup. Following a Davis Cup doubles match against Serbia and Montenegro Davis Cup team, Murray was penalized for cursing at the umpire, Adel Aref. After the game, Murray declined to shake hands with the umpire.

Following the investigation into Nikolay Davydenko, Murray asserted that match-fixing is an issue in tennis and that everyone is aware that it occurs. Rafael Nadal and Davydenko also disputed Murray's statements, but Murray insisted that they had been misinterpreted.

In a June 2015 column for the French sports publication L'Équipe, Murray criticized what he called a "double standard" applied by many in their attitudes toward Amélie Mauresmo in her capacity as Murray's coach. Murray highlighted how many observers attributed his poor performances during the early part of her tenure to her appointment, which Murray denied, before pointing out that his previous coaches had not been blamed by the media for other spells of poor form. In addition, he bemoaned the absence of female tennis instructors in the professional game "Am I turning into a feminist? Well, if being a feminist means working for women to be treated equally to men, then I think I have succeeded ". Regarding women's tennis, Murray has frequently corrected others.

Murray responded when BBC broadcaster John Inverdale said that he was the first tennis player to win more than one Olympic gold medal, saying, "I suppose Venus and Serena have won maybe four each." Murray has also stated that prize money for male and female tennis players should be equal.

Regarding the decision by the United Kingdom to exit the European Union, Murray has not expressed his viewpoint. However, he voiced his astonishment at the outcome of the UK referendum after winning Wimbledon in 2016, saying that "it's vital that everyone gets together to make the most of it."

ANDY MURRAY'S PRIVATE FAMILY LIFE

Andy Murray, a tennis champion, is regarded as one of the greatest sports figures to ever represent the UK. Off the court, the Scottish athlete is a self-described family guy. His stunning partner Kim Sears is frequently seen courtside supporting her husband among Wimbledon's most illustrious visitors.

Andy plays tennis at home at his $5 million Surrey house when he's not squaring off on Center Court. The celebrity is supposedly preparing to move into a brand-new five-bedroom home that will reportedly have a tennis court, swimming pool, massage room, and gym when it is finished. It will be situated on a 28-acre estate and have a courtyard-style garage structure to house Andy's collection of vehicles and provide his expanding family plenty of room.

At a US Open party in 2005, Andy first met his wife Kim. Kim was on the road at the time with her father Nigel, who oversaw the women's division of the English Lawn Tennis Association.

Although their romance grew swiftly, the pair was able to keep it a secret as they got to know one another.

Teenage sweethearts when they first met

A year later, in San Jose, California, hopeless romantic Andy won his first championship and sped through the spectators to kiss his gorgeous new fiancée. Kim was suddenly thrust into the spotlight.

She was still an adolescent attending school at the time. She later remembered, "I left with him thinking it's okay because he's never going to win so I'll be back in time for school on Monday and then he did!

Andy kissed his wife Kim secretly at Wimbledon in 2013

"You need to phone in and let them know I have the winter vomiting sickness and I won't be in," she recalled telling her mother, "but then it was on the front cover of the paper so I was busted." You are swooning; we are not.

When was Andy Murray's wedding?

On April 11, 2015, the pair exchanged vows, and Kim looked every inch the blushing bride as she made her way down the aisle in a custom Jenny Packham gown adorned with Swarovski crystals.

Loud applause greeted Kim as she pulled up to Dunblane Cathedral in a stylish silver vintage automobile. She then unveiled the white dress fit for a queen with a long skirt, elbow-length sleeves, and an open V-shaped back. Kim was 27 at the time.

In 2015, Andy and his radiant wife Kim were married.

After six years of marriage, the happy pair still prefers to keep their private life hidden from their admirers, but Andy, the devoted husband, still sometimes posts an Instagram snapshot of his stunning wife.

When he posted a charming picture of Kim and their two border terriers, Maggie May and Rusty, the former world number one referred to his girlfriend as one of his "three favorites"!

Has Andy Murray ever had kids?

Together with his wife Kim, the Wimbledon winner has four kids: Sophia, age 6, Edie, age 4, Teddie, age 2, and a girl who was born in March 2021.

He provided a rare glimpse into their hectic home life with four kids running around the house in an interview with Alison Hammond.

Maggie May and Rusty, two border terriers, are part of Andy's family.

The actor revealed, "Seeing the kids sit at the table, behaving, eating their food, and go to bed at the correct time, that kind of thing makes me pleased."

Sophia, who is five years old, has already shown an interest in athletics, according to Andy, 34. "If my oldest daughter wanted to play tennis once a week, I'd be fine, but at their ages, it's crucial to be doing something with their friends," I said.

Andy Murray had his fourth kid when?

During the lockdown, it was discovered that Kim had quietly given birth following a very secretive pregnancy, making the adoring father a father of four. When asked if they had a boy or a girl, the tennis star first opted not to say, but it was subsequently revealed the pair had a daughter.

Part Two

THE COACHING CREW

Who Is Andy Murray's Coach

Andy Murray, a Scot, is the first tennis player in history to successfully defend a gold medal at two Olympic Games, the player with the most Queen's Club Championship titles, and one of the finest players on the Tour. On May 15, 1987, Andrew Barron Murray was born in Glasgow, Scotland. His mother, Judy Murray, and elder brother Jamie, who is also a professional tennis player competing on the doubles tour, served as his initial coaches. His father is William Murray. At the age of three, Andy's mother took him to play tennis on the neighborhood courts. At the age of five, he participated in his first competition against other players, and by the age of eight, he was playing in the Central District Tennis League. He had football aptitude from an early age and was requested to train with Rangers Football Club at their School of Excellence when he was 15 but turned it down to concentrate on his tennis career. He then joined The Big Four, a group of players that dominated men's tennis in the 2010s, proving that he had made the right choice. All-court player Andy Murray is renowned for possessing one of the Tour's greatest and most reliable two-handed backhands. For revitalizing men's tennis in Great Britain after the early 20th century. His favorite tennis player is Andre Agassi, and he supports Arsenal and Hibernian in football. Early in March 2022, Andy announced that he will be teaming up with Ivan Lendl, one of the living giants of this sport and his old coach who helped him achieve tremendous success on the Tour.

Ivan Lendl

Ivan Lendl

Ivan Lendl, a former professional tennis player who is recognized as one of the best of all time, was born on March 7, 1960, in Ostrava, Czech Republic. He is also referred to as the "Father of Modern Tennis" and is credited as having a major effect on the current popular playing style of aggressive baseline power tennis. He invented a new technique of hitting strong forehands with high topspin. Ivan won 94 singles matches throughout his playing career, including eight Grand Slams. He was the first player to compete in 19 major finals, and for 270 weeks, he held the singles world no. 1 ranking. He won six titles in doubles. 1994 saw his retirement.

He began his coaching career with Andy Murray at the beginning of 2012, and it has been said that he helped Murray become more responsible and reliable. Andy won the Brisbane International to get the season off to a strong start. reached the Australian Open semifinals, won the Wimbledon Championship, and won the Olympic gold medal on the same court a few weeks later, becoming the first British man to accomplish it since 1908. In the longest final in the history of the competition, he defeated Novak Djokovic to win the US Open, the final Grand Slam of the year. Murray concluded the year as the third-ranked player in the world, and as a result of his performance, he was made an officer of the Order of the British Empire.

Andy started the 2013 season by defending his Brisbane International crown and making it to the Australian Open final. Later, he captured his second Miami Masters championship and debuted at No. 2 in the world. Murray won his third championship at Queen's Club to kick off the grass-court season, and he later won Wimbledon to become the first British champion since 1936. His choice to get back surgery ended his season early.

Lendl and Murray split up in 2014, then they got back together in June 2016.

He's a powerful leader with a lot of experience, but Murray also noted that we had shared many comparable situations. "I've won games when you may anticipate a pat on the back but receive the reverse. Additionally, I have occasionally lost games and received the compliment, "You played wonderfully,"

Since their June reunion, Murray may have enjoyed his finest season ever. By defeating Juan Martin Del Potro in the Olympic gold medal match, he won his fifth AEGON Championship, the Wimbledon Championship for the second time, and the Rio Olympics. By winning the China Open, Shanghai Masters, and Erste Bank Open, he extended his winning run. After winning the Paris Masters for the first time, he went on to win the ATP World Tour Finals after the year and climb the world rankings to No. 1.

For the first time, Murray received this accolade as the International Tennis Federation named him the 2016 ITF Men's World Champion.

The 2017 season was by no means a triumph for Murray, in contrast to the previous one. At the Dubai Championships, he only garnered one victory and endured a nearly year-long hip ailment. He and Ivan Lendl announced that they had again mutually terminated their coaching relationship after the season.

Andy competed in the Stuttgart Open final and cracked the top 50 for the first time since their third reunion in March 2022.

"Ivan being on my squad helps. We know each other well, we've had a lot of success together in the past, and he still has faith in me. There aren't many instructors and other people who have done this over the past few years, but he has. Murray told the media.

In addition to Andy, Ivan Lendl coached Alexander Zverev throughout his career from August 2018 to July 2019. Alexander defeated Novak Djokovic, becoming the first player to defeat the current World No. 1 player, to win the Washington Open and the ATP Finals, demonstrating the rapid impact of Lendl on the field. Due to unsatisfactory performance in 2019 and personal reasons, they parted ways after Zverev only won the Geneva Open since the season started in 2019. Lendl was reportedly less interested in professional coaching and more focused on his dog or golf skills.

ANDY MURRAY'S PAST COACHES

The coaching staff at Murray has seen significant transition over time. He was tutored by Leon Smith from 1998 to 2004 when he was a little child.

Leon Smith

Leon Smith

Glasgow, Scotland is where Leon Smith was born in 1976. He competed in national junior tennis competitions, but he never became a pro. At the age of 18, he started coaching professionally at the club level. He later became Tennis Scotland's national performance officer and an LTA Master Performance Coach. He has been the Great Britain Davis Cup captain and men's tennis director since 2010. Andy won the Orange Bowl in 1999 and 2001 while being coached by Murray, and in 2003 he began competing on the Challenger and Futures Circuit. At Glasgow Futures, he won his first senior championship. He afterward won at Xativa, Rome Futures, and the 2004 Junior US Open. He was named the BBC Young Sports Personality of the Year later that year. Smith and Murray remained close friends, and he occasionally helped Murray later in his career. Andy traveled to Barcelona as a young and aspiring footballer to train at the Sanchez-Casal Academy under the direction of Pato Alvarez.

Pato Alvarez

Pato Alvarez

Pato Alvarez, who was born in Medellin, Colombia, on December 15, 1934, passed away this year at the age of 87. He won the Colombian national championship eight times throughout his career. His best Majors finish was in the third round at the French Open. He moved to Spain in the 1970s, where he established the country's current tennis training program and rose to fame as a tennis instructor. As the technical manager of the Royal Spanish Tennis Federation in the 1980s, he was in charge of selecting the top Spanish tennis players to represent Spain in the circuit's major events. He mentored notable tennis players on the world stage including Andy Murray and Juan Monaco as well as exceptional Spanish rackets like Emilio Sanchez Vicario.

Murray broke off his relationship with Pato Alvarez in April 2005, citing his unfavorable demeanor.

Andy selected Mark Petchey to be his coach in April 2005.

Mark Petchey

MARK PETCHEY

In Essex, England, on August 1, 1970, Marc Petchey was born. He received his education at the exclusive Forest School in northeast London. His father, Rod, served as his first coach. In 1988, he went pro, and in the Nottingham Open, he only won one doubles championship.

On the hard courts at Aptos and Binghamton, Murray won Challenger competitions under his direction.

In an interview, Petchey stated of Andy, "Andy is a remarkable sportsman who should be recognized nationwide for his devotion and particular abilities.

Murray and Brad Gilbert teamed up after Petchey.

Brad Gilbert

Brad Gilbert

Brad Gilbert was born in Oakland, California, on August 9, 1961. At age 4, he started playing tennis after watching his father, Barry Gilbert, take up the game. Gilbert began competing on the professional circuit in 1982, winning 20 solo championships and reaching career-high singles rankings of No. 4 in 1990 and No. 18 in doubles four years earlier. He has taught several elite athletes after leaving the tour, most notably Andre Agassi, Andy Roddick, and Kei Nishikori.

Gilbert was the coach of Andre Agassi for eight years, from March 1994 to January 2002. Agassi won six of his eight majors when Gilbert was his coach. Gilbert was said to by Agassi as "the best coach of all time." On June 3, 2003, Gilbert was appointed Andy Roddick's coach. Under Gilbert's direction, Roddick won the 2003 US Open, secured the 2003 year-end world number one ranking, and advanced to the 2004 Wimbledon final. It was revealed in December 2010 that Gilbert will return to coaching and team up with Japanese player Kei Nishikori for 15 events in 2011. After the 2011 season, Gilbert and Nishikori's collaboration came to an end.

He won the San Jose Open at the beginning of his partnership with Andy, defeating a top-10 player for the first time and rising to the position of British No. 1. Murray concluded the 2007 season ranked No. 11 in the world after winning the San Jose and St. Petersburg Opens.

Andy began the 2008 season by mentoring Miles Maclagan.

Miles Maclagan

Miles Maclagan

In Zambia, Miles Maclagan was born on September 23, 1974. At the age of 12, he began playing tennis in the United Kingdom, where he eventually rose to the singles and doubles the level of 172. He was a member of the team that won the Australian Open Doubles championship in 2005 and served as a mentor to doubles experts Wayne Black and Kevin Ulyett. He also coached Borna Coric, Laura Robson, Sam Stosur, Marcos Baghdatis, and Phillip Kohlschreiber. He helped Baghdatis win the doubles title at the 2012 Zagreb Indoors.

By winning the 2008 Doha, Marseille, and St. Petersburg Opens and making it to his first Grand Slam final at the US Open, Andy had a successful start to the season with Maclagan. His final season ranking was No. 4 in the world. Andy won the Doha Open to start the 2009 season, followed by victories at the Rotterdam Open, Miami Masters, and his first championship at Queen's, Montreal, and Valencia Open. He took over and kept the No. 2 spot in the rankings throughout the year, but he concluded the year as the No. 4 player in the world. "When we first met, I had a lot of respect for Murray, and throughout the year, especially the last few months, that regard has only increased. It has been amazing to witness it firsthand. He is competitive in many areas, not just on the tennis court. He manages to go in there and charges himself up," Maclagan added.

They split up after a few disappointing performances in the first half of 2010.

"Andy hired me to share my thoughts, but he didn't entirely agree with these, so here we are. When they broke up, Maclagan remarked, "I think in any organization you need to be clear in the path. We knew if we didn't come to an agreement we might be where we are now. Alex Corretja was the replacement coach who Murray quickly hired.

Alex Corretja

Alex Corretja

On April 11, 1974, Alex Corretja was born in Barcelona, Spain. Since 1991, he has competed as a professional tennis player, winning three doubles championships and seventeen singles titles. He won the first-ever Davis Cup with Spain, the Italian Masters, the Indian Wells, and the ATP World Tour Championships, among other events. He started teaching when he retired in 2005 and is currently employed by Eurosport as a field interviewer at Grand Slam competitions as of 2015.

After making contact with Corretja, Murray successfully defended his Canada Open title, followed by victories at the Shanghai Open and Valencia Open, where he won his first doubles championship with his brother Jamie. March 2011 marked their breakup.

After losing in the French Open quarterfinals, Andy created history by hiring Amelie Mauresmo as his coach, making her the first woman to ever train a top-ranked male tennis player.

Amelie Mauresmo

Amelie Mauresmo

Amelie Mauresmo was born in Saint-Germain-en-Laye, France, on July 5, 1979. When she was four years old, she picked up tennis after seeing Yannick Noah win the 1983 French Open. She achieved World No. 1 status in 2004 and won 25 singles championships, including one Wimbledon and one Australian Open. She retired in 2009 after fifteen years in the professional world. She has been the French Open's director since 2021.

Andy won the Shenzhen, Vienna, and Valencia Opens in 2014 while being coached by Mauresmo. Murray said that Jonas Bjorkman would serve as his head coach through the conclusion of the season when she notified him in 2015 that she was expecting and would be taking maternity leave.

Jonas Bjorkman

JONAS BJORKMANC

In Alvesta, Sweden, on March 23, 1972, Jonas Bjorkman was born. Jonas Björkman, the son of tennis instructor Lars Björkman, started playing the sport at the age of six. He was well-known for his doubles performance, where he was World No. 1 and won 54 trophies, including nine Grand Slams. Playing alone, he only garnered 6 victories.

While Bjorkman and Murray were in training together the rest of the year, Andy won his first clay-court championship at the Munich Open, followed by another at the Madrid Open. He later won the Montreal Open, his fourth Queen's title, and helped Great Britain win their first Davis Cup championship since 1936. After the season, they ceased working together, and in 2016, Andy and Mauresmo jointly announced that their coaching relationship was over.

Dani Vallverdu, Jamie Delgado, and Jez Green served as Andy's training partners and assistant coaches throughout his career, and Jamie Delgado also served as a fitness coach.

EIGHT THINGS WE LEARNED FROM MURRAY DOCUMENTARY

One of the greatest sporting tales of 2019 is Andy Murray's journey from his sad declaration that his career was likely to end following major hip surgery to winning an ATP championship less than a year later.

A behind-the-scenes documentary called Andy Murray: Resurfacing, which will start airing on Amazon Prime on Friday, now exposes the British former world number one's emotional odyssey over the previous two years.

His Childhood Experiences In Dunblane Led To Anxiety

When Thomas Hamilton murdered 16 children and their teacher in March 1996, Murray, 32, was a student at the neighborhood elementary school. Murray was a native of the Scottish village of

Dunblane. When the tragedy struck, he hid in the headmaster's study.

Murray discusses the tragic events of that day, as well as other upsetting family events, which have influenced his life. Murray knew the shooter.

The three-time Grand Slam winner eventually replies to director Olivia Cappuccini's earlier question on why tennis is important to him in a stirring late-night audio mail.

He confesses to Cappuccini, Murray's brother-in-boyfriend, law's "Obviously I had the situation that happened at Dunblane, when I was approximately nine," in December 2018.

"For every one of the kids here, I'm sure it would be challenging for a variety of reasons. We knew the man since we attended his kids' club, drove him to and left him off at various locations, and he had been in our car " Then, a year later, our parents were divorced. Children are struggling because they can observe this but may not fully comprehend what is happening.

Then, six to twelve months later, my brother Jamie left the house as well. He left to practice tennis and went away. Naturally, we used to accomplish everything jointly. The fact that he moved away was difficult for me as well. I experienced a lot of worries throughout that period and for almost a year after that, which was noticeable when I was playing tennis. When I was competing, my breathing would become quite problematic. Because all of these issues are taboo and we don't discuss them, tennis serves as a form of escape for me.

"I can still be that kid thanks to tennis. It is significant to me for this reason."

He believed his career was about to end, which is why he started crying in Washington.

After having his initial hip surgery in January 2018 and making a hesitant recovery later that year, Murray underwent a more complicated resurfacing procedure in January of this year to get relief from the ongoing chronic pain.

One of the most memorable scenes from the first comeback was when the Scot slumped down in his chair, covered his head with a towel, and cried hysterically on the court for many minutes after defeating Romanian Marius Copil in the third round of the Washington Open at 3:02 a.m. local time.

The whole scope of his mental condition is now revealed to us. He realized then that his professional life was about to end.

He states: "I was extremely, terribly sad after the match because I feel this is the end for me" in a video message shot at 5:09 am in the American capital.

My body simply doesn't want to do it, and my mind is no longer willing to endure the discomfort.

I had hoped that after 16, or 17, months, I would feel better.

"I simply felt like I was going to an end, so it was an emotional night. That makes me sad because even though my body is telling me to stop, I want to keep going. I'm sorry, but I'm unable to continue because it hurts.

After a "bleak" Christmas phone chat, his wife Kim advised him to resign.

Murray said he was experiencing "zero happiness" when playing tennis during a particularly challenging training block in Miami before the end of 2018.

In a phone call that she characterizes as "very gloomy," he phones his wife Kim, who was at home in London.

She says, "He constantly wanted someone to tell him to stop, and I tried to explain that nobody could since he decided to make." "I understood what he was calling for and that's what he wanted," the speaker said. As I was setting up the Christmas tree, I remarked to him, "You're not pleased; you said you'd give it till Christmas. Call it a day."

He almost opted out of the emotional announcement of the Australian Open In January, an emotional Andy Murray worried that the 2019 Australian Open would be his final competition. Although Murray had privately believed he was nearing the end, he had offered few hints publicly, so his emotional declaration at the Australian Open's pre-tournament press conference caught everyone off guard.

Murray admitted the Grand Slam in Melbourne may be his final competition, but he believed he could play through the agony until Wimbledon before quitting tennis.

However, he continued to question whether he should divulge everything the morning of his scheduled admittance.

Two hours before speaking to the media, he declares, "I'm going to say something today, I know I'll become emotional."

"But I frequently alter my mind. I had to make a statement.

Despite having little to no discomfort in his hip that morning, Murray reports feeling frightened, nervous, and having butterflies in his stomach.

He explains, "I want my leg to feel incredibly painful while deciding that.

That raised questions. He then gives his physiotherapist, Shane Annun, a call. Murray adds, "I think I'm making a mistake."

His surgeon warned him of the dangers of
making a tennis comeback

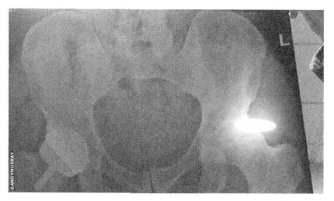

Murray posted this picture on Instagram of his hip following surgery

Murray ultimately decided to have the resurfacing procedure performed at the London Hip Unit by famous surgeon Sarah Muirhead-Allwood, who had previously treated the Queen Mother.

In a post-surgery discussion, Murray expresses his concern that returning to tennis might result in more hip damage and require surgery.

She says, "What if I told you that if you started playing top-class tennis again, I think you've got a 15% chance of destroying the hip in the first seven years."

Murray giggles uneasily.

"It's not a case of it will or it won't, that's how it works." Chances exist. Would you be willing to run the risk of seven years of tennis?"

Murray said he was content with being pain-free and having a fresh lease on life, so he originally had doubts about returning to the court.

But his mother Judy foresees a shift in that.

"He must have unfinished business, according to my instinct. I'm not being duped, "She claims.

He watched a gruesome video of the hip surgery

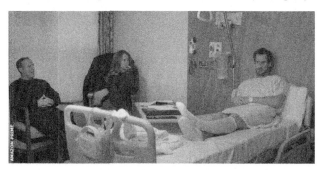

Murray is visited by fitness instructor Matt Little and his wife Kim while he is in the hospital.

There are no restrictions on viewing the video of Murray's two hip operations.

We watch graphic footage of his procedure with Australian surgeon John O'Donnell in the opening moments of the movie, and Murray evaluates his scar, concluding that it looks "quite great."

We show him afterward seeing a graphic video of someone else undergoing that procedure after he decided in January of this year that he wanted to have his hip resurfaced.

He quips, "I find it hilarious that they're using a hammer."

Soon later, he is undergoing the surgery. The camera records everything that happens from the minute he lies down on the operating table, including gruesome shots of bleeding equipment working on the joint within open skin.

Murray remarks dryly when he emerges from surgery, "Running around a tennis court is not a smart idea.

Wife Kim jokes that the filmmaker has to record the comment because they know the subject would change his mind - again. They are joined by fitness instructor Matt Little and physiotherapist Annun.

He has a bromance with his physio

The funniest and lighthearted parts of the movie revolve around Murray's "bromance" with Annun.

Murray says, "I'd have so much fun being married to Shane.

Mark Bender, another physio, described Annun and Murray as "an elderly couple that knows precisely what buttons to press," adding that Murray enjoys preying on Annun's vulnerability of being "gullible."

When Murray begins his physical therapy following the second hip operation, the pair's friendship is once again depicted in a heartwarming and humorous scene when Murray expresses his love for the physio.

"I can hold Shane and he can't move away from me because otherwise, he would hurt my hip, which is a genius benefit of having a painful hip. He cannot pull away from my embrace, "He giggles.

These conversations highlight Murray's razor-sharp sense of humor and his penchant for "winding up" his crew. Murray's sardonic humor is mostly directed against Bender because we discover that he goes by the moniker "Slender."

Murray chuckles, "It's amusing since he's not very slim.

Murray won the European Open last month by defeating Stan Wawrinka, marking his first ATP Tour singles victory since March 2017.

He used to sense hostility toward him.

When Murray revealed at the Australian Open that his storied career appeared to be coming to an end, he received an outpouring of support from all corners of the globe.

But he didn't feel it until recently, after winning Wimbledon, the Olympics, and the Davis Cup, which furthered his popularity with the British people.

According to his wife Kim, "He did believe there was a certain level of enmity towards him."

"He would likely acknowledge that there is a lot of love in the world today.

I occasionally have to pinch myself over what he did.

I can't believe I saw that take place."

Part Three

THE RIVALRY

Tennis - Is Andy Murray, Novak Djokovic the last great rivalry today?

These days, it's advantageous to be a couch potato tennis devotee. That is if you like the storied rivalries that have developed, deteriorated, and then reemerged during the previous ten years. Given the extensive paths that today's gamers have taken, the finest content this game has ever seen has been dumped upon us.

But this era is currently going through a little refurbishment phase. Although the level of magnificent tennis has spoilt us, we are currently seeing something we haven't seen in 10 years.

The Stan Effect, should we say.

You are aware of the subject at hand. Naturally, Stanislas Wawrinka. He became just the second non-member of the elite big four to capture a Grand Slam since 2005. However, this trophy stood for something greater than Wawrinka's success. It exposed a certain frailty in the top players of the game that we hadn't seen in earnest in over a decade.

Given how long the present domination has lasted, it almost seems unbelievable that any kind of disbandment would be approaching a court near you. Roger Federer started a journey that would become his enduring legacy in 2003. Whether we win or lose, we are firmly rooted in a generation where the entertainment value is on par with exceptional outcomes.

We were left with a rather unsettling question as the two 26-year-old competitors in the main event, Novak Djokovic and Andy Murray, emerged from the entrance smoke in a crowded Madison Square Garden on Monday night. Are they the last chance to continue this age of dominance?

Earlier this week, Murray stated on a conference call, "I mean, we've played in quite a few significant ones over the previous several years."

We've also played some fantastic matches in Australia, but from my perspective, that was my first Grand Slam, and the way the match played out — where I was up two sets to love and he came back to win that — was probably my finest one versus him.

If you think we're ruling out more incredible performances from Roger Federer and Rafael Nadal, we most definitely aren't. But when you take into account the beating his legs suffer, Nadal is a dog year older in terms of on-court experience than Djokovic and Murray.

Federer performed well this past week in Dubai to win his first tournament of the year, but his performances have fallen in recent years, particularly last year when he lost in the second round at Wimbledon and the fourth round in New York. The two major four older statesmen have suffered setbacks. Nadal, who missed 712 months of action in 2012–2013, and Federer, whose erratic back and abrupt Slam failures have been acknowledged. Age, injury, or both will eventually catch up to them. It must, surely?

Murray and Djokovic were born just seven days apart, and their extensive, fascinating past promises many more captivating moments.

We've competed against each other since we were 11 years old, so we've known each other for a very long time, Murray said on Monday. "We've played each other in some of the greatest events in the world including the Grand Slam," Murray said. I believe that the athleticism in tennis has changed, and having played against Novak and experienced what it's like to play against him on the other side, I know that he is an incredible athlete and moves exceptionally well. So our games have changed a lot; we have grown up a lot.

But Murray and Djokovic have also experienced difficult periods.

Wawrinka eliminated Djokovic from the Australian Open earlier this year, and then Federer defeated the world No. 2 in Dubai. Only two of the previous nine tournaments have been won by Djokovic, who won three Slams in 2011. When comes Murray, who lost the Australian Open to a specific 17-time Grand Slam champion after finishing 2013 on the operating table to treat a bothersome back injury.

Roger had a fantastic tournament in Dubai, according to Djokovic. He may be ranked No. 7 or 8, but regardless of that, he has won 17 Grand Slams, is one of the greatest players in game history, and you can never sign him out.

You have to be at the top of your game to beat him because he always plays well, regardless of the surface you are playing on. Rafa is present, of course, as well as young players like the great servers Jerzy Janowicz, Milos Raonic, and Grigor Dimitrov. Roger Federer is the player across the net. It's too early in the season to predict who will place first or who will win Grand Slams, but I think more players than just the four Americans are now capable of doing so.."

The issue of the ceiling comes next. Djokovic, has he attained his? He won three major championships in 2011, but just two in the previous nine. Cause for concern? At the US Open in 2012, Murray ended a career oh-for, and he naturally delighted his local audience by winning Wimbledon the previous year. Murray's game isn't as strong as it was six months ago, though, as seen by his mediocre 12-4 record and one quarterfinal appearance in four tournaments.

Raonic, Dimitrov, and Janowicz are farther on. Are they prepared to sabotage prime-time television? The Stan Effect—is it real? Dare we suggest that the repulsive P-word, parity, is gradually encroaching on the game? Or is everything merely a quick diversion? The future?

There appear to be a lot of questions and few solutions.

But one thing is certain: Two months into 2014, there is still no certainty. What we can say is that we should enjoy what we're witnessing because, sooner or later, when Djokovic, Murray, and their big-four colleagues are no longer in control, the game may head into obscurity, which will be difficult for the couch men to watch.

THE RIVALRY BETWEEN ROGER FEDERER AND ANDY MURRAY

Given that the two players have only met in three grand slam matches—with Federer winning twice and Murray only once—there is no obvious answer to this query. However, some people view Murray's victory over Federer in the 2012 Olympic semifinal match as a more meaningful triumph.

Andy Murray and Roger Federer have dropped 11 of 25 games. He overcame the Swiss four times in four triumphs, although he lost in the 2009 ATP Finals and the 2010 Australian Open final. Comparable to a better record versus Nadal and Djokovic is one against Federer. Federer won the championships in the next three sets at 5-7, 6-3, and 6-4. They defeated the Swiss in their subsequent five matches, winning four of those matches in straight sets.

Murray and Federer have faced off 25 times, with Murray taking home 11 victories to Federer's 14. In their first 10 encounters between 2005 and 2009, Andy Murray and Roger Federer squared off six times, with Murray winning six of the games.

Andy Murray won the Rogers Cup final against Novak Djokovic on Sunday in Montreal, securing a place in the US Open. He defeated Andy Murray in four sets, 6-4, 4-6, 6-3, to claim the title. For the first time since the Wimbledon championship in 2013, he triumphed against Djokovic, snapping an eight-year losing run.

In 2012, he won his first Grand Slam competition at the US Open.

He has won the Wimbledon Men's Singles title twice. His first championship came in 2013, a year after he lost to Roger Federer in the final when he defeated Novak Djokovic in straight sets. Murray won the coveted title by defeating Milos Raonic in three sets for the second time.

How frequently did Murray face Federer?

25 times on tour, the most recent meeting taking place in Cincinnati in 2015. Murray hasn't faced the No. 1 player in the world in the competition since over a year ago (in Madrid in 2016).

At Wimbledon, Andy Murray has participated 14 times. Australian Duckworth was beaten by the Americans in the first round. This page contains all the information you need to know about a tennis player. On May 15, 1987, Sir Andrew Barron

Murray OBE was born in Glasgow, Scotland. Twice, Andy Murray has won the Wimbledon championship.

He won his first championship in 2013; the same year, he also advanced to the final. Murray placed first or very close to first in eight of the nine final rankings.

The Scotsman spent most of the time between July 2008 and October 2017 in the top ten. On the ATP Tour, Andy Murray has amassed 46 singles victories, including 14 on the ATP Masters 1000 circuit. In 2012, he triumphed in the US Open for the first time. In 2013 and 2016, Wimbledon won two championships. He was the first British male to win the Davis Cup in 2015, which was Great Britain's first triumph since 1936.

Two of the greatest tennis players of all time, Djokovic and Murray have one of the sport's most captivating rivalries. Djokovic has defeated Murray in 36 games, winning 25 of those games overall and 11 of those games in finals. The Serb not only owns the record for most victories in a year but also has eight Wimbledon crowns to his name. In addition to those two victories, he also won the US Open in 2013 and the Australian Open in 2007. The top-ranked tennis player in the world right now is Novak Djokovic of Serbia. In contrast, Murray is rated second to Nadal. When Djokovic won the 2005 Australian Open, their rivalry officially started. Since then, the two have faced off in 19 straight grand slams, with Andy taking home five trophies and Novak capturing 12 championships.

The rivalry between Andy Murray and Novak Djokovic is one of the most exciting in tennis history. Both teams compete against one another ferociously, and their rivalry will only intensify over time.

Wimbledon's undisputed champion is Andy Murray.

On the grass courts, the British superstar has enjoyed a remarkable career, making the finals in all but one of his outings. Nadal and Murray have faced off five times, with Murray coming out on top four times.

Who Has Beat Federer the Most Times?

This question does not have a single, conclusive answer. Over the years, Roger Federer has played a variety of players in several tight encounters. He has had some remarkable victories as well as some catastrophic defeats. It is challenging to determine who has defeated him the most times as a result.

A player who has dominated Roger Federer throughout the match overwhelms him on Centre Court. He was defeated in straight sets by eight-time champion Waldemar Hralkacz of Poland, who also took the title. The 39-year-old Federer was asked if it was his last Wimbledon participation, to which he responded, "No, but I hope so."

He said that he did not completely discount the notion. Polish tennis coach Craig Boynton needed time to heal following a Covid-19 match earlier this spring. The Swiss tennis player made his Wimbledon debut in 1998, and after defeating Pete Sampras in the championship match in 2001, he shot to fame. For the first match since he was a youngster, Roger Federer lost in the third round of the All-England Club. The Center Court partisans raised their voices when Federer started to falter.

Since making his professional debut in 1998, Roger Federer has won 17 Grand Slam tournaments, making him the all-time leader in that category. Federer has made four prior appearances in the Masters 1000 event final, but he has never taken home the trophy. Roger Federer silenced his detractors in 2017 by winning several titles, including the Australian Open, US Open, and Wimbledon. Many have questioned if he has participated in too many events and has previously struggled in important tournaments. The legendary tennis player Stan Wawrinka is presently preparing in Switzerland for the 2020 Tokyo Olympics, where he and Croatia's Marin Cilic are considered the front-runners for the Men's Tennis Silver medal. One of the most decorated Olympians in Olympic history, Federer is the most successful male tennis player thanks to his eight Wimbledon victories. Federer is a sporting superstar who set several records at Wimbledon. His achievements will be remembered for the rest of his career.

Federer vs. Murray Wimbledon

The Murray vs. Federer battle at Wimbledon was fantastic. The game was tight and they both gave it their all. Murray ultimately prevailed, and it was a fantastic triumph.

Wimbledon is a tennis competition, but for Andy Murray and Roger Federer, it's unique. Eight different winners have been crowned on the grass courts at Windsor Park, and Murray is a particular fan. Due to the epidemic, interviews are held in a small, isolated room with no extra space. Roger Federer: I utilized my resources to the fullest. The game wasn't supposed to start until 40. In 2019, he came close to winning Wimbledon (but lost by a whisker). Now that the event has been suspended for two years and the 2020 edition has been abandoned, Wimbledon has changed.

Since August 2015, Andy Murray and Roger Federer have not engaged in a competitive match. Murray sported a Tartan cap to their last encounter, which took place at a charity show in Glasgow, and Federer donned a kilt. They didn't get along well at first, but as time went on, their bond deepened. However, Matteo Berrettini defeated Murray in the second round of his exhibition match.

Swiss Maestro Andy Murray

Andy Murray, a Swiss maestro and one of tennis' greatest players, plays the game. He has two Olympic gold medals and three Grand Slam singles victories. In addition, he is the first British player in 77 years to win the Wimbledon men's singles championship.

Andy Murray loses to Roger Federer in the ATP Masters championship match. We've had enough of Andy Murray. Federer easily prevails, handing the British their second consecutive loss. Murray defeated David Ferrer in Group B last night, and he will now play Robin Soderling in the semifinals. He didn't resemble the competitor who had beaten him in the Master's Cup's opening round in Shanghai a month earlier. Federer played a faultless tactical performance, emphasizing consistency and establishing his tempo rather than largely depending on his offensive style.

ANDY MURRAY, ROGER FEDERER AND NOVAK DJOKOVIC'S RIVALRY, FAMILY LIFE AND FRIENDSHIP

They have combined for 63 Grand Slam titles and have produced some of the greatest tennis moments in history. The Big Four — Andy Murray, Roger Federer, Novak Djokovic, and Rafael Nadal — will partner up on the court for this year's Laver Cup competition rather than competing against one another.

These tennis greats are adversaries on the court, but their camaraderie extends beyond Grand Slam matches. They have not only competed against one another on the tennis courts for more than 20 years, but they have also helped one another behind the scenes.

Andy discusses his strong relationship with Rafael and how the Spaniard's impact on him motivated him to travel to Spain as a youngster in this exclusive interview. Andy is a two-time Wimbledon winner.

Despite acknowledging that it might be challenging to compete alone on the Grand Slam circuit, Serbian champion Novak has moved his attention from himself and his profession to his children since becoming a parent.

Fatherhood has evolved as well. Andy admitted openly that he now finds defeats to be slightly easier. The group is prepared to help Rafael, 36, who will become a parent for the first time this year, along with Roger.

Following Roger's statement last week that he is retiring from tennis, this eagerly awaited tennis competition will be extra special.

The tennis legends will be joined by Casper Ruud and Stefanos Tsitsipas as a member of Team Europe. Björn Borg will serve as the team's captain, and Thomas Enqvist will serve as vice-captain.

Team World's Felix Auger-Aliassime, Taylor Fritz, Diego Schwartzman, Jack Sock, Francis Tiafoe, and Alex De Minaur, who will be accompanied by captain John McEnroe and his younger brother Patrick McEnroe as vice-captain, will give the athletic superstars a tough fight.

I met down with Andy, Roger, and Novak before the Laver Cup to discuss their relationship, their love of tennis, and how being fathers has impacted them.

Have there ever been times when, despite your history as rivals, you needed each other's friendship or support personally?

Roger: Absolutely. In my more than 20 years on the tour, I've been fortunate to make friends and face off against a wide range of players and coaches. I intentionally try to connect with other players off the court and at training to assist them as much as I can despite the stress and pressure of games and tournaments. The Laver Cup is unique because of this link, among other things. The Laver Cup is a unique chance for teamwork and allows us to exchange professional and personal thoughts with one another that we would never be able to do in a conventional tournament environment.

For this year's Laver Cup, Roger Federer is present.

Novak: A few years back, Roger and I got the chance to play together in Team Europe, and it was a lot of fun. I found it enjoyable to spend time with people without being in direct competition. I admire Roger both as a renowned tennis player and for the ideals, he upholds in his family. While we were having a mini-event dubbed "Breakfast with champions," Roger graciously sat next to me and supported the work of my charitable organization at the time.

Due to your intense emphasis on individual accomplishment, might it get lonely playing professional tennis?

Roger: No, in my view. We all share the desire to succeed, but even more so, we recognize that teamwork in the locker room benefits the sport that gives us the chance to participate and make a difference.

How essential is it to you as a professional tennis player to have friends you can depend on? Men frequently find it tougher to discuss the value of friendships and connections.

Andy: Professional players must cope with a lot of pressure and great expectations to succeed on the field, as well as the additional burden of being in the public spotlight, which I had to get used to starting at the age of 16 and didn't find easy. Because of this, it has always been crucial for me to have a network of dependable friends and family members.

Andy Murray smiles in preparation for his Laver Cup match.

Novak: It is highly significant. We travel frequently, and the majority of us do it alone. Being alone is not simple. I respect my buddies because of this, and I always search for opportunities to help other gamers. Their relationship has meant a lot to me, especially when they have openly stood by me while I was going through a difficult moment.

How does it feel to play the game as a team rather than as a competitor?

Roger: Working as a team with my biggest competitors is exciting. It was an incredible experience to play doubles with Rafael [Nadal] for the first time at the Laver Cup in Prague. Having guys like Rafa on the court with me is always a joy and an honor. Aside from that, it's something I genuinely like. The team dynamics mix competitive fervor with a special energy that enables us to verbally and physically express our love for the sport. Anyone would be enraged by Rafa's display of passion while sitting on the Team Europe bench since it makes him appear to be cheering for Real Madrid at the Bernabéu Stadium.

Andy; I adore participating in team sports. Tennis can be a lonesome sport at times, and I think that as singles players, we don't get to play it nearly enough. Team competition in tournaments like the Davis Cup and the Olympics is something I truly look forward to. I've heard wonderful things about the Laver Cup, where I'll be competing for the first time, and I'm looking forward to joining forces with some of my competitors.

Supporting one another at the Laver Cup

Novak: The prospect of rejoining Team Europe is quite thrilling. Being able to play in a team situation with players you're usually fighting against, along with joining Rafa, Roger, and Andy, three of my biggest all-time opponents will be one of the rare occasions in our sport.

Do you get to see a different aspect of each other as teammates?

Roger: Throughout a tournament, there is always a feeling of tension and friendly competitiveness on the field and in the locker room. When former adversaries work together, you see a different side because you have the same objective. We encourage one another. In practice, we encourage and support one another. The level of concern shared by everyone is astounding and motivating. We are inherently fierce competitors, so having allies who comprehend the difficulties better than anyone else in your camp gives you a great incentive to battle for the team.

After the 2022 Laver Cup, Roger made retirement plans public.

Andy: Yes, we'll all put in a lot of effort together to try to extend Team Europe's winning run!

Novak: Being a part of the same team allows you to support and boost one other up, which is extremely pleasant.

Tell us anything about your friendship with another player on your Laver Cup squad that might surprise us.

Andy: Since we were young, Rafa and I have had a close friendship. We've grown up in competition together and hearing about his training set-up in Spain was a critical time for me. I contacted my mother that evening to let her know I had made up my decision and I was moving to Spain since he was able to practice so much more than I could and hit with Top 100 players when he was 14 or 15. I knew right away I would have to adjust my setup in the UK!

What would you choose if you could combine your abilities to make the perfect player?

Roger: Because there are so many dynamics to take into account while evaluating any talent, this issue is quite challenging to answer. There are several forehands (defensive, attacking, running, etc.) and volleys, for instance (transition, set, finishing, etc). Making a choice is made much more difficult when you consider the various surfaces. Since there are so many of these talents to develop to improve your game, I believe this is what makes tennis so beautiful.

During The Laver Cup, Roger And Novak Demonstrate Their Tennis Prowess.

Andy: The combination of Rafa's forehand and Novak's backhand would be rather potent. I would also borrow John Isner's serve because I am aware that he has previously represented Team World and possesses a respectable serve. I'm hoping my lob will occasionally be useful.

What activities do you guys engage in behind the scenes during significant competitions?

Roger: Our free time is devoted to matching preparation at important events. To ensure that we are in the greatest possible physical and mental positions, we collaborate closely with our teams. I also want to balance my time between being with my family and friends. I like visiting and seeing the intriguing locations where we have the opportunity to compete when it is practical.

Posing with the Laver Cup tennis ball is Novak Djokovic.

Andy: At an important tournament, you shouldn't be doing too much away from the court, so I try to unwind as much as I can while I'm not in court. I obviously try to watch as much tennis as possible, but I also enjoy playing fantasy sports (basketball and football), so I'm frequently planning my next signings and trash-talking in WhatsApp chat groups. I try to stay in touch with the family as much as I can give how frequently I'm on the road.

Novak: I genuinely love spending time with my children. I adjust to meet their requirements and, for once, I am just a parent, and that feels incredibly humble. Additionally, labor is rather difficult.

How has becoming a father altered you?

Roger: Being a father has given me a completely new perspective on my values and how I view the world. My life revolves around my family and kids. I am appreciative of the knowledge and experiences we may gain from one another. Along with the wonderful experiences we get to enjoy when we visit beautiful locations and spend time with amazing people, it is satisfying to establish and grow our home life.

For Andy, this will be his first Laver Cup.

Andy: It significantly altered my life because tennis was my top priority before becoming a father. After every defeat, I would also get depressed. I've been able to establish a better balance as I've aged. Don't get me wrong, I still detest losing, but the lows are short-lived since my kids always manage to cheer me up.

Novak: The changes that becoming a father has brought about in me are continual and persistent. I advance along with them. Together, we develop. Before them, I and my job were the only things the family cared about. They have become the center of our attention since they entered our lives, and I consider this to be the nicest thing to have ever occurred to me. I now value everything I do and have more, especially my time. I devote all of my leisure time to them. My heart may have gotten bigger as well.

Are there any words of wisdom you can give Rafael as he prepares to become a father for the first time?

Roger: Enjoy the now. While you will always cherish your Grand Slam victories and professional successes, your family will soon bring you new feelings and celebrations on a deeper level than you could have ever dreamed.

Rafael and Roger had been pals for several years.

Andy: Get some rest right now! He's in a wonderful stage of his life, and since he's a laid-back, peaceful individual, he'll be OK. You need a lot of patience, but you can't imagine your life without them since it's the finest thing in the world.

Novak: just to maintain an open mind and develop alongside the child. We can learn so much from them! What a delight that trip has been; I can't wait to watch Rafa and Xisca as parents. Again, many congrats from my family and I!

The Past Few Years Have Been Tough'

A bit of advice: decline any dinner invitation from Sir Andy Murray. Although he may be the most successful British tennis player in contemporary times, it's safe to argue that he isn't the best cook of his time. Murray's only area of expertise? Pasta with Dolmio sauce stirred in.

Thankfully, we don't converse across his kitchen table—we do it on Zoom. His curly hair is surprisingly under control even though he is at the National Tennis Centre in Roehampton during the last moments of lockdown (his wife, Kim Sears, cut it). The 33-year-old is a cheery company and appears healthier than ever while donning a pec-hugging hoodie, but this hides a four-year period during which the two-time Wimbledon champion has been plagued by injuries.

Murray has been primarily off the court as a result of this, but he hasn't slowed down. Instead, he has focused his energies on brand-new endeavors, such as AMC by Castore, a partnership with the upscale sportswear company, and appearing in the documentary Andy Murray: He resurfaced during the lockdown and gave birth to his fourth kid. In addition, he is attempting to get back into the top tier of tennis after falling from No. 1.

Murray is a surprising expert in fashion. He acknowledges that he is not quite Karl Lagerfeld, despite once having lunch in Paris with Dame Anna Wintour, the American Vogue editor (she made no comments about his wardrobe). But he is aware of his preferences and what athletes require.

He explains in his distinctive Scottish monotone, "I don't know anything about fashion at all, but I trial and test all of the kits from the technical side of things." When anything is presented to me, I can tell if I like it or not.

His participation with Castore goes beyond merely lending his name to a new line—having previously worn Fred Perry, Adidas, and Under Armour—as he has invested in the company. Performance is the focus, with a clean, basic look. There is a chance he will wear it this summer at Wimbledon, where he hasn't competed in the singles competition since 2017.

Murray had hip surgery three and a half years ago. He underwent a second, more invasive hip resurfacing treatment after an unsuccessful return and found it difficult to put on socks. Only 25 competitive games have been played since by the player whose game is built on deft movement and quick pace.

But as anyone who has watched Murray's career will know, he welcomes challenges. He attained the pinnacle of the sport that epitomizes summer despite being born in Dunblane, Scotland, where there are only on average 3.4 hours of sunshine every day. He has always had to deal with the limits of his body after being diagnosed at the age of 16 with a split kneecap that many believed would prohibit him from competing at the top level. He has demonstrated good judgment by winning two Wimbledon championships, a US Open, and two Olympic gold medals. But he readily admits that the last years have been challenging.

Murray admits, "Once I got the metal hip, I realized it wasn't going to be simple." There are just occasions when I didn't anticipate it to be this way.' Murray has been working hard in the gym but is hardly able to play. But he persisted anyhow. I still want to play, therefore I have to either do it or stop. I simply no longer find it as enjoyable as perhaps I did a few years ago.

I still desire to continue playing. Just not as much as maybe I did a few years ago, I guess.

Murray has been able to spend more time with his young family, which has been an advantage of the forced time away from the tour.

"I spent a lot of time with my kids over a previous couple of years and got to develop fantastic relationships with them, something I wouldn't have had the opportunity to do otherwise. I got to witness my kids grow up." That has been the wonderful outcome of this in some respects.

Murray is the most approachable of the "big four" male tennis players (together with Roger Federer,

Rafael Nadal, and Novak Djokovic). He cries in agony whenever he misses a shot that he believes he should make. Like other parents, he tried to find activities for his kids to do during the lockdown. The children liked the cardboard castles I was making, but I thought they were ugly.

Murray is distinguished not just by his down-to-earth demeanor but also by the respect he enjoys among his contemporaries on both the men's and women's circuits. This is not typical among tennis politics, at least not for those who pay careful attention. Murray received a flood of sincere accolades from female players following his original retirement announcement in 2019, including Billie Jean King, who referred to him as "a champion on and off the court."

Murray had no intention of championing equality. But he spoke out against injustice and sexism when he observed them. I became aware that there was an issue when I began working with a female coach, Amélie Mauresmo, and I was like, "Wow," you know she's been number one in the world? There is no greater success than that. I believed she was being disparaged in the media only for being a woman.'

Winning Wimbledon in 2013

Murray has also not hesitated to take on journalists who fail to mention female athletes' records. "I simply want everyone to be treated equally, including men and women." That is not radical in my opinion; I only believe it ought to be a human right. The Association of Tennis Professionals' initial reluctance to comment on serious allegations made against two male players, Alexander Zverev (who has been accused of domestic violence by a former girlfriend) and Nikoloz Basilashvili (who is awaiting trial in Georgia on a charge of domestic violence against his ex-wife), has also been a target of his. He is prepared to challenge this organization. The claims have been refuted by both men. I believe that ATP waited far too long to respond. A blind spot is that we don't have any procedures or protocols in place for when claims like that are made.

'I simply want both men and women to be treated equally. That doesn't strike me as radical.

This composed yet outspoken Murray did not enter the global scene in a completely fledged state. For every international sports star, scrutiny is the cost of doing business. He arrived at his current position as a national treasure in the Attenborough mold by taking the scenic path. I was a little child who enjoyed playing tennis but was accustomed to receiving no audience or attention at all.

When I first began doing news conferences, I very much spoke everything that was on my mind, and it was thought to be entertaining and thrilling. But after that, I started to have problems with jokes that were misinterpreted. When asked who he was rooting for at the 2006 World Cup of football, he jokingly said, "whom England was playing against." For years, he was troubled by this comment. I was 20 years old when it happened. At that age, you are still learning about the world, and you don't know who you are. During that time in my job, I didn't love what I was doing or all the things that came with it as much.'

Murray's style has been compared to an intricate structure intended to hide the reality that it lacks the one element necessary to dominate, a point-ending forehand, according to journalist Steve Tignor. It's one of the reasons his three main competitors have won many more majors. However, statistics alone cannot adequately express Murray's significance to the game or his standing as a national hero.

Regardless of the outcome of this return, his professional, if not gastronomic, legacy is assured.

FUTURE MIGHT NOT EVEN INVOLVE TENNIS'

The tennis star discusses the joys of family life, his desire to win Wimbledon for a third time, and what lies ahead.

After a 40-minute delay, Andy Murray finally arrived on Court Number 3 at Wimbledon. It is lunch, not the rain, that is to blame. not

262

strawberries, but sushi. There are two reasons to be relieved as he sets up for our shot while dressed in a navy suit and a sweater the color of the SW19 sky.

One: He's here and willing to accommodate us throughout the grass court season, which is his busiest time of the year. Two: His life doesn't operate with the unnerving precision that his team's Saturday itinerary, which said that he wasn't scheduled to eat until 3:50 pm, implied. Who can object to the two-time Wimbledon winner taking a short break after a morning of grueling training?

Murray addresses the crowd of onlookers, including his agent, Telegraph's stylist, Wimbledon officials, representatives of American Express (of which Murray is an ambassador), and even a group of teenage groundskeepers, saying, "This was the first court I ever played on at Wimbledon."

As an 18-year-old, he entered his first competition in 2005 and made it as far as the third round. He then went on to win the championship in 2013 and 2016. He tells me later off-court that he visits this place frequently during the year, but "I don't feel the chills or the butterflies every time. I do when the competition is going on. The location has changed. It has a distinctive vigor. I am more knowledgeable about the tournament's past now.

For Murray, the previous few years have been about attempting to recover his passion for the sport after dealing with excruciating agony that at times prevented him from walking, as well as his world-class form after having his hip replaced in 2019.

Now injury-free, Murray is upbeat about the upcoming Championships. He suffered from stomach agony during the final in Stuttgart two weeks ago, and he lost despite twice having treatment on the court; now, he is philosophical about the blows he has received.

Injury has made for a trying trip, but it has also reminded him of why he loves the game. "Yes, I'd love to be back at the top of the global rankings and I want to win Grand Slam tournaments once more, but it is not the main reason I play or the reason I took up tennis. No kid ever takes up sports for that reason.

He's come a long way from the young man who used to drive his minivan down from Dunblane to see the game. He is one of the Big Four players that have dominated tennis for 10 years and has won Grand Slam championships against players like Novak Djokovic, Rafael Nadal, and Roger Federer.

The fact that he is the only one permitted to stand on the sacred grass today just serves to emphasize his faraway star status. This southwest London suburb's perception of him is similar to peering at a statue of a Greek deity from behind a rope. Maybe I'm being intimidated by the 35-year-reputation olds for being a little glum.

I stage whisper, holding the photographer's light reflector and avoiding Murray's direct sight, "Can you tell Andy to smile?" Perhaps a negative aspect of his personality? He does, however, recognize the humor in things and isn't beyond making jokes about himself (see his Instagram).

As we return to the hospitality suite, the interview begins as the clock is running out. I've been told not to say anything "political" by his PR people. It's challenging because he may rightfully be expected to comment on both the Wimbledon ranking point suspension and the Texas high school tragedy as a

Wimbledon winner and a resident of a community that has been devastated by a dreadful school massacre.

Although he was quite open with the media at the start of his career, Murray has not always had a good relationship with the press. They appreciated the fact that I wasn't like Greg Russki and Tim Henman and was just saying whatever came to mind. answering all inquiries without considering the impact of my words."

Afterward, a couple of words were misconstrued or said out of context. "I suddenly began to lose some faith in that connection. I used to get anxious before interviews because I didn't want to say the wrong thing. I now feel a little more at ease with that aspect of the situation."

I simply spoke whatever came to mind. What has changed is that he now feels more comfortable avoiding topics he doesn't want to discuss. "I know how to maneuver around the subject to not get myself in the headlines if I don't want to be," he said. "I used to answer every question without thinking about the repercussions of what I said."

Today's interview is intended to focus on Murray the person, the father of four children, rather than merely the godlike athlete and the most successful tennis player from the UK since Fred Perry.

Murray's 2019 documentary does a fantastic job of demonstrating his tenacity as well as his dry humor, illuminating why Murray is sometimes referred to as the funniest man on the ATP circuit.

The world was able to watch the brutal emotional toll of moving from being the top player in the world to facing the very real threat of early retirement within the span of a season, as well as the teamwork that supports a singles star.

There's little question that he feels more at ease opening out to tennis fans about some aspects of his life. His Instagram is now filled with pictures of him playing tennis, wearing a dragon onesie, and going to Disneyland. One aspect of that transition seems to be fatherhood. The four children he and his wife Kim have are Sophia, age 6, Edie, age 4, Teddy, age 2, and Lola, age 1.

One benefit of participating at Wimbledon is getting to sleep in his own bed, and he will be one of the few athletes eating a home-cooked supper with his family while chatting about topics other than the day's match. He states, "I think the support system surrounding athletes is incredibly crucial. Now that there is more attention being paid to mental health, it is being discussed that optimum performance does not always result from spending four months away from friends and family. There is an other perspective that could be more fruitful.

He will find it just a little bit simpler to shut off after he departs the site during the tournament and travels the short distance home to Surbiton.

He is aware that as soon as he leaves his hotel room when attending other competitions, he will run across other players and coaches. "You spend the entire time talking about tennis."

While other clubs in sports like football and cricket have tight rules around family time, Murray accepts it as a part of his professional path. "I wouldn't be able to continue playing if it weren't for my wife and my family's support. My wife continues to support me in my training and in my efforts to accomplish my goals. Murray's career has been heavily supported by women.

What's it like to have a mother who is almost as well-known as he is? " My mother is a really unique individual. She consistently puts in too much work.

She never slept much while we were youngsters. She would get up in the middle of the night and work on stuff like emails.

In 2013, Andy Murray posed with his mother Judy Murray at the InterContinental Park Lane Hotel at the Wimbledon Championships Winners Ball.

She adores both her job and tennis. She exudes a level of vitality that I am unable to equal with my own kids. But I suppose she may return home after that. (Judy will confess that she experienced sexual assault in 2014 following our conversation. Andy, who was not informed of the event, would claim that he was "upset and outraged... There should be no tolerance for that kind of behavior anyplace.

When he was a child, it was the same. His and his brother Jamie's early vacations were spent at places like Centre Parcs, where they played sports like tennis, golf, football, table tennis, and gymnastics thanks to their active parents. He was competitive because of the milieu in which he was raised. "I don't think being more competitive than the next person is something you are born with," said the speaker. When he first started competing at age six, Andy would always lose because of Jamie's 15-month advantage because of having an elder brother.

"He was stronger, more intelligent, and superior in every way. I believe I occasionally observe that with my children. The second child detests losing since it is all she has ever known.

In a 1998 photo taken in Edinburgh, Scotland, Andy and his brother Jamie are shown participating in the Scotland vs. England under-12 tennis match.

He has no doubt that his parents' selflessness is what led to his and Jamie's athletic achievements. Two young people from Scotland had little chance of becoming elite tennis players. At the age of 12, my brother moved away to attend school. Nothing is worse in my opinion than sending my children away when they are 12 or having them attend boarding school. When I was fifteen, I visited Spain. Jamie visited France when he was 16 years old. Our parents had to make these enormous financial sacrifices. Thus, we were really lucky."

Many people complain about tennis parents who are overly intrusive and engaged with their kids, but I can perfectly understand how that may happen, Murray explains. When your child is 10 years old, you spend all of your weekends and holidays around the nation to assist them. However, when they get 18 and the governing bodies try to get involved, they occasionally don't do a fantastic job of helping the parents. Some individuals just state, "I don't want to deal with parents."

He sounds as though he is referring to Emma Raducanu. It's quite challenging. I've never gone through what she did, where your life changes in an instant. But he has empathy. It's hard to determine whether everyone who becomes engaged with you is acting in your best interests. You are aware of your family's intentions for you. The family will undoubtedly make blunders since everything is new. When I was younger, I would have worked with management firms in addition to instructors who might not have been the best fit for me. Do they desire what's best for you or do they just want to profit greatly from you, is the inquiry you ask. It's quite difficult to navigate.

For the record, if the chance arose, he would dearly want to play doubles alongside Raducanu. "Unfortunately, there are no true mixed doubles competitions outside of the Grand Slams."

Tennis is already being played by Murray's two oldest kids once a week for 45 minutes. Although he brings kids along, his current priorities are for them to enjoy sport and gain life and self-awareness lessons rather than copy his actions.

Despite the recent difficulties he has had, Murray is still some distance from being a full-time tennis father. He hasn't felt this well in years until the last four months. "I've had time to play, practice, and train. I'm crossing my fingers that I'm in a good position for the upcoming weeks.

He had never been an injured player until his hip problem. Though I'll definitely go get one now, I'd never had a muscular problem, he quips. He attributes that to consistently keeping up his physical fitness and flexibility in addition to his training. Not to expect a physio or doctor to repair you is his advise to laypeople. Yes, a physiotherapist can temporarily improve your symptoms, but only physical training and building up your body's resistance to stress can prevent the injury from returning.

He played at Roehampton for two hours and 20 minutes before to our shoot and interview. Along with seeing his physio, he worked out in the gym. Although he always challenges and pushes himself, he acknowledges that during the last 20 minutes of practice, he wasn't satisfied with himself. He admits, "I was in a pretty foul attitude when I arrived here. I told my coach, and he said that wouldn't happen tomorrow. That won't help me with my desired outcome, which is, you know, trying to win Wimbledon.

Even if his body isn't always cooperative, the Murray I've encountered is still just as motivated and as competitive as he ever was. He could play a lengthy match at the age of 24 and then feel good the next morning. "Now that I do it, I feel awful."

As an alternative, he makes an effort to give himself "the best opportunity to feel well," which includes having a decent night's sleep: "For me, it comes first." He consults with a nutritionist who prescribes the precise amounts of protein and carbohydrates he must eat. "I make sure I have the correct quantity of fuel and am well hydrated."

For the first time since he was a child, he engaged in extensive road biking while in lockdown and developed a competitive spirit. It doesn't imply that you beat your previous time every week. Although you shouldn't always beat your score, it's important to keep a personal record and strive for personal improvement. I don't always consider the neighbor's cycling skills or the number of Grand Slams they have won. I've always had a rivalry with myself.

He claims that what distinguishes him today is that "I don't only live in a tennis bubble. I am aware of what is happening elsewhere in the world.

I do inquire about the shootings in Uvalde. "What's happened is obviously horrible, and I don't understand the resistance to make changes in that nation," he responds gently. Why not give something new a shot? After Dunblane, it was successful here. If it doesn't work, go back, but at least try a different approach."

We're running out of time fast. Where is he at this moment in his life? He enjoys both fatherhood and golfing. Although he can't paint and draw as well as Kim, he enjoys art, much to the dismay of his kids.

"I have hobbies and interests outside of tennis, and I am certain that everything will be good when I ultimately finish. It won't come to an end. As opposed to when I was 25, and even even at the start of the documentary in 2017, when I was still a little like that.

On July 10, 2016, Andy Murray celebrates his victory over Canadian Milos Raonic in the men's singles Wimbledon Championship final at the All England Lawn Tennis Club in London.

He will always engage in physical activity if only to maintain the strength of the muscles surrounding his metal hip. I'll always keep up a fantastic strength and conditioning routine, going to the gym four to five days each week for 45 to an hour each time.

He emphasizes that the finest announcers were frequently not the best players and that he is not very interested in the broadcasting side of things. "Many players only watch the Grand Slams and don't pay much attention to the circuit."

So, after 15 years, where will he be? "Coaching has always attracted me. There's also a risk that I won't play tennis anymore. Although I now believe that I will always be involved in tennis in some capacity, there have been periods when I have neglected the sport and have not followed any of the competitions. I just have the kids at home during that time. That part of things is rather intense.

Time is running short, and more sponsorship obligations are coming up. In addition, there is a package of half-eaten sushi, a competition to prepare for, and children to take care of. Despite his busy schedule, Murray seemed content to return for whatever life throws at him.

Andy On Getting Kids Into Sport

I believe that encouraging my kids to do sports is a good thing. Tennis isn't a guarantee, though!

Kids should get involved in team sports as early as possible. When we were young and lived in Scotland, my mother was particularly good at it. We felt like a team since Jamie and I were a member of a group of young players who rode about in a van.

There are many excellent life lessons that sport provides. The topic of participation medals is a big one. I don't like that. However, I do believe there are lessons to be learned from not always succeeding. We don't always succeed in life. It all depends on how you handle such setbacks. You can learn from your mistakes and the times when things didn't exactly go your way. Along with being an effective team player. Even if you don't participate in sports as an adult, many employers value it.

When one of your team members does something, you realize that pointing the finger at them won't solve the problem. Being supportive and talking to them at those times is crucial. I want my children to participate in sports because I want them to win Wimbledon.

Once a week, I take my kids to play tennis, and I like to see them do that. When your children decide this is what they want to do professionally, it is a very different sacrifice. All of a sudden, you have to put a lot of sacrifices forward. My brother and I didn't understand why our parents would alter their schedules to accompany us to activities.

At Wimbledon, I ran into a member whose children, who are now nine and ten, also play tennis. She informed me that weekends are now spent taking the kids to tennis matches, much like her parents did for her. I won't name her.

She then said, "I detest it. I want to take a vacation or unwind on the weekends, but tennis constantly gets in the way!

LONG WAY FROM NO 1 BUT STILL MAKING PROGRESS

Andy Murray claims that after holding the World No. 1 ranking, success is measured by that.

Murray, who fought his way back into the top 50 in the previous year, hasn't had the finest year by that metric.

Despite the gradual development, Murray is nonetheless encouraged by how he has sometimes performed.

He aims to advance farther in 2023 and maybe put an end to his six-year championship drought on the ATP Tour.

Murray stated, "When you've been at the top of the game and gone to No. 1, that's always where your reference point is in terms of how you're performing." In that regard, it has been quite average, but at the start of the year, I was rated No. 135 in the world, and now I am in my 40s. Given the size of the leap, this year has been fine. Therefore, that would be quite advantageous for many participants.

"I would have liked to have performed better, and I don't think I've played my greatest tennis this year," the player said. This year has been alright. I'm hoping to continue improving throughout the coming year.

Dan Evans, another Brit, is attempting to go beyond the scope of his abilities. "I approach these competitions differently than many of these elite players; I need a lot of things to go my way, but making it to the semifinals in Montreal proved that, with the appropriate preparation and tennis, I can advance to the latter rounds of these competitions. Murray hopes to travel to Florida to finish his preseason workouts and get his physical work in before the season starts. "I can improve, and that's why we're on the practice courts every day, and it's just about tinkering," Murray said.

"I've talked a lot about the summer and the things I want to accomplish with my team, and you know, I've got that plan in terms of where I'm going to do it," the speaker said.

I'm heading to Florida, you know, for the first time in a while, and I used to always spend my offseasons there, working very hard on my game and getting physically fit. I just want to keep moving forward. I've come a long way from where I was this year, so if things start to go backwards, like performances don't get better or my physical health deteriorates, I'll have to take a closer look at things, but I'm still kind of moving in the right direction and have plans for a successful year next year.

Printed in Great Britain
by Amazon

28006680R00165